Select Soccer Drills

WALTERS

John A. Reeves, EdD
State University of New York at Stony Brook
J. Malcolm Simon, MA
New Jersey Institute of Technology

Leisure Press
Champaign, Illinois

Library of Congress Cataloging-in-Publication Data

Reeves, John A.
    Select soccer drills / John A. Reeves and J. Malcolm Simon.
        p.   cm.
    Includes index.
    ISBN 0-88011-408-8
    1. Soccer–United States–Training.   I. Simon, J. Malcolm.
    II. Title.
    GV943.9.T7S5   1991
    796.334'0973–dc20   90-38919
                                                                                              CIP

ISBN: 0-88011-408-8

Copyright © 1991 by John A. Reeves and J. Malcolm Simon

Acquisitions Editor: Brian Holding; **Developmental Editor:** June I. Decker, PhD; **Production Editor:** Valerie Hall; **Assistant Editors:** Dawn Levy, Kari Nelson; **Copyeditor:** Barbara Walsh; **Proofreader:** Phaedra Hise Hargis; **Production Director:** Ernie Noa; **Typesetter:** Kathy Boudreau-Fuoss; **Text Design:** Keith Blomberg; **Text Layout:** Denise Peters; **Cover Design:** Jack Davis; **Cover Photo:** Billy Stickland/Allsport; **Illustrations:** Asdrubal Franco, Gretchen Walters; **Printer:** Versa Press

Leisure Press books are available at special discounts for bulk purchase. Special editions or book excerpts can also be created to specification. For details, contact the Special Sales Manager at Human Kinetics.

Printed in the United States of America   10

Leisure Press
A Division of Human Kinetics
Web site: www.humankinetics.com

United States: Human Kinetics, P.O. Box 5076, Champaign, IL 61825-5076
800-747-4457
e-mail: humank@hkusa.com

Europe: Human Kinetics, 107 Bradford Road, Stanningly
Leeds LS28 6AT, United Kingdom
+44 (0) 113 255 5665
e-mail: hk@hkeurope.com

To Christine, Melanie, and Stephanie
and
to those who will have
a positive influence on youth

Contents

Foreword

John Reeves and Mal Simon have done it again. Having already authored two widely acclaimed coaching manuals of soccer drills and soccer-related games, they have reached the climax of their combined 60 years of successful coaching and dedicated service to soccer with their new book, *Select Soccer Drills*.

The book presents the best of the best. It includes drills used by coaches of championship-caliber high school, college, and university teams and state-select and United States Olympic development teams.

Designed for all levels of coaching, *Select Soccer Drills* is so well organized that it can be easily used by players and coaches at any level of ability and experience. It includes basic drills for coaches and players with little experience as well as complex drills for experienced coaches and advanced players. The indexes of drills categorized by title, focus, and contributors are extremely useful.

Select Soccer Drills will be valuable to beginners and experts and is a must for every soccer coach's library.

Jerry Yeagley
Head Men's Soccer Coach, Indiana University

Preface

As the most popular game in the world enters the 1990s, excitement and anticipation abound: Player participation has increased dramatically in youth programs at all levels worldwide. The most recent participation statistics indicate that more and more young people are playing this safe, inexpensive, and creative game. Competitive participation has experienced similar growth.

Along with this explosion in soccer participation has come the need to develop more and better prepared coaches. Coaches are urgently needed to work not only with the increased number of participants but also with athletes capable of competing on a more sophisticated level. We recognize this challenge and believe that our book will meet it. *Select Soccer Drills* picks up where our earlier publications, *The Coaches' Collection of Soccer Drills* and *The Soccer Games Book*, left off. Our new book reflects the most recent approaches to teaching soccer techniques and tactics. It draws from a diverse group of contributors: coaches of high school boys' and girls' teams and men's and women's college teams, and coaches who have played and coached on national and international levels. We believe that using *Select Soccer Drills* along with our earlier publications will give coaches, both neophyte and experienced, the best planning resources for organizing worthwhile practice sessions.

The importance of drills cannot be overemphasized. Before a coach can expect a player to perform a skill, that skill must be taught through adequate practice. Once the player learns the skill, he or she can then perform it competently, even in pressure situations. However, achieving this level of performance requires much practice, with planned progression from simple to complex movements. Well-planned drills are the best means for such development and provide the player with a firm foundation for future learning.

It is not enough to use one, two, or even a few favorite drills over and over again. Players become more proficient if they are not bored by a lack of variety in the practice program. *Select Soccer Drills* provides a variety of drills to supplement each coach's personal favorites. All of the drills were contributed by successful coaches and have sustained the test of time.

To make it easier to use the book, information necessary to effectively organize each drill is included in its heading. Directly below the title, from left to right, are the focuses (listed in order of importance), and the recommended playing area, number of personnel, and type of equipment.

We are grateful to those coaches who contributed to *Select Soccer Drills*. We also thank Jerry Yeagley, head soccer coach of Indiana University, for his endorsement. We are indebted to Joan Sauer for her assistance in gathering the drills; to Munjal Desai, a New Jersey Tech graduate assistant, for his patient instructions on the use of the Macintosh; to Asdrubal Franco, a soccer player and architecture major at New Jersey Tech, for drawing the diagrams; and especially to Mary Monaco, who has worked so diligently with us in the preparation of all three books.

Drill Finder

Accuracy Passing Under Pressure

FOCUS	AREA	PERSONNEL	EQUIPMENT
Passing Agility Fitness	20 × 20 yards	6 players	2 balls

FORMATION: Four players (X1-X4), one in each corner, are in a 20 × 20 yard grid. Another player (X6) is in a "horse" position in the middle of the grid, next to the working player (X5). X1 and X3 each have a ball.

PROCEDURE: X1 passes the ball in the direction of X6. X5 jumps over X6 and plays the ball to X2. As soon as this pass is made, X3 passes the ball in the direction of X6. X5 jumps back over X6 and plays the ball to X4. Play continues in this fashion for 45 to 60 seconds; then all players rotate positions.

VARIATIONS: 1. Play one or two touch.
2. Use the inside or the outside of the foot.
3. Move servers closer and have them serve with their hands for volley kicks.

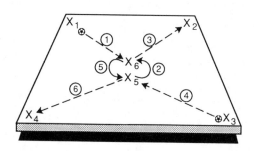

CONTRIBUTOR: Stephen Locker, Men's Coach, University of Rochester, Rochester, New York

Across-Field Warm-Up

FOCUS	AREA	PERSONNEL	EQUIPMENT
Basic skills	Full field	16+ players	1 ball for each
Warm-up			2 players

FORMATION: Players are divided into two equal groups. The first group stands along a touchline, and each player faces a partner in the second group, which is lined up 5 yards away on the field of play. Each player in the second group holds a ball.

PROCEDURE: The players holding balls jog backward across the field, making easy air tosses to their partners. The partners jog forward, receive the balls in the air, and return them to the throwers. When the opposite touchline is reached, the partners reverse roles and return to the other side. Each time across the field one of the following skills is performed:

1. Receiving the ball with the inside of the foot (alternate left and right)
2. Receiving the ball with the instep (alternate left and right)
3. Catching the ball on the thigh, dropping it to feet for return to thrower
4. Catching the ball on the chest, dropping it to feet for return to thrower
5. Heading back to the thrower—thrower should make the receiver do some jumping headers

VARIATION: Reverse the direction of the thrower and the receiver—that is, the thrower jogs forward, the receiver backward.

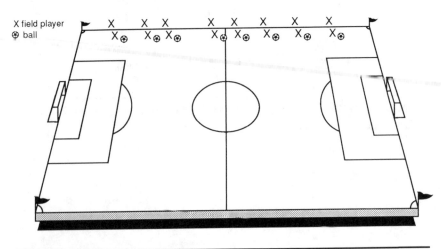

X field player
⊕ ball

CONTRIBUTOR: John Makuvek, Men's Coach, Moravian College, Bethlehem, Pennsylvania

Air Balls

FOCUS	AREA	PERSONNEL	EQUIPMENT
Passing	Circle with	An even	1 ball for each
Receiving	20-yard	number of	2 players
Warm-up	diameter	players	Vests

FORMATION: Players form two groups: One group is outside the circle, each player with a ball in hand; the other group is scattered inside the circle.

PROCEDURE: Players inside the circle check away and then move to any player with a ball, calling out the name of a body surface (e.g., chest, thigh, right foot). Each player on the outside tosses the ball to the approaching player, who settles the ball with the correct body surface and plays the ball back on the ground to the same player. Inside players continue moving to other players, repeating the drill but using different body surfaces. Play continues for 1 minute; then inside and outside players switch positions.

VARIATIONS: 1. Players control and pass without the ball touching the ground.
2. Allow only one touch back to the outside player.
3. Add a third player to pressure the player receiving the ball.

X field player
- - - ▶ pass
———▶ sprint
⊕ ball

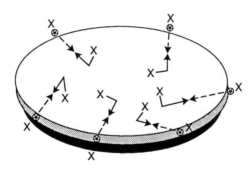

CONTRIBUTOR: Jim Felix, Men's Coach, SUNY at Stony Brook, Stony Brook, New York

Attack vs. Defense

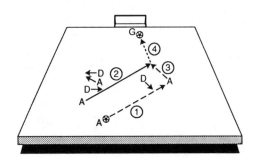

FOCUS	AREA	PERSONNEL	EQUIPMENT
Attack	30 × 30 yards	8 players	1 ball
Defense			1 goal
			3 vests

FORMATION: Four attackers and three defenders are positioned randomly within a 30 × 30 yard area. The defenders wear vests. One of the attackers has a ball. A goalkeeper is in the goal.

PROCEDURE: The object of the drill is for the attackers to exploit their numerical advantage and finish with a shot on goal. The attackers move the ball, looking for the open player and holes in the defense. The defenders will gain experience in how to cover a one-down situation. The ball is given back to the attackers following a shot on goal or defensive interception.

VARIATION: Increase the number of attackers.

A attacker
D defender
G goalkeeper
– – –➤ pass
------➤ shot
——➤ sprint
⊕ ball

CONTRIBUTOR: Peter Matischak, Assistant Men's Coach, Seton Hall University, South Orange, New Jersey

Attacking End Line

FOCUS	AREA	PERSONNEL	EQUIPMENT
Attack	1/2 field	14 players	7 balls
			8 cones
			2 goals
			6 vests

FORMATION: Using half the field, place one goal at midfield facing a goal on the end line. Using four cones on each side, create a 10-yard-wide channel along each touchline. There are two teams: Each has one player in each channel, four players in the middle, and a goalkeeper. One team wears vests. A player on one team has a ball. Extra balls are behind each goal.

PROCEDURE: Play four vs. four in the middle area and one vs. one in either channel. For a team to go to goal, the ball must be served from a channel. When the ball is in a channel, play one vs. one until one of the players breaks into the offensive end of the channel. At this point the defender becomes passive to allow the cross. The four attacking players in the middle organize near post, far post, trail, and supporting runs while the four defenders cover. Play is continuous.

VARIATIONS: 1. Vary the pressure in the channels; if there are not enough crosses, eliminate opposition in the channels.
2. Using wall passes, takeovers, or overlaps, players in the channels can exchange places with middle players.

G goalkeeper
X, Y field players
⊛ ball
⊓ cone

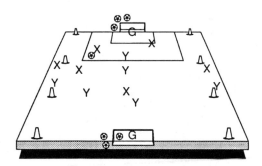

CONTRIBUTOR: George Perry III, Men's Coach, St. Bonaventure University, St. Bonaventure, New York

Attacking From Midfield $\boxed{6}$

FOCUS	AREA	PERSONNEL	EQUIPMENT
Attack	2/3 field	12 players	1 ball
Support		1 coach	10 cones
Shooting			2 goals
			5 vests

FORMATION: Using the cones, divide the field into thirds. A goalkeeper, two defenders, and two attackers are in the defensive third, with four attacking midfielders and three defenders in the middle third. The defenders wear vests. The coach, with a ball, is outside the middle third touchline.

PROCEDURE: The coach starts play by serving the ball into the middle third area. If one of the three defending midfielders gets the ball, the defenders play keep-away. If one of the four attacking midfielders gets it, the attackers penetrate and attack immediately. The player with the ball finds and passes to an attacker in the attacking third. The passer goes to support so the play is three vs. two in the attacking third; or the closest player or the player furthest away supports.

VARIATIONS: 1. The number of players can increase or decrease.
2. This drill can emphasize defensive tactics as well as attacking.

A attacker   D defender   AMF attacking midfielder   ∿⟶ dribble   ┈┈┈▶ shot   ⊕ ball
C coach   G goalkeeper   DMF defending midfielder   ╌╌▶ pass   ──▶ sprint   ⟁ cone

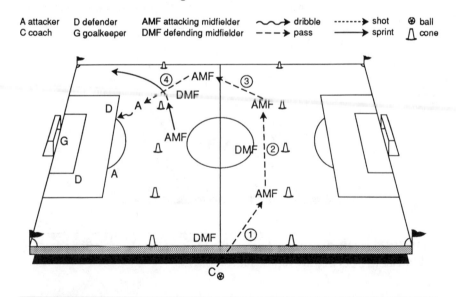

CONTRIBUTOR: Bill Barfield, Men's Coach, The Citadel, Charleston, South Carolina

Attacking From the Back

FOCUS	AREA	PERSONNEL	EQUIPMENT
Passing	Full field	14 players	12 balls
Control			2 goals
Shooting			
Turning			

FORMATION: Two groups with six players each line up outside diagonally opposite corners of the field. Two players are in the center circle. A goalkeeper with six balls is in each goal.

PROCEDURE: The goalkeepers begin the drill by simultaneously throwing a ball to the first player in each line, who is moving upfield. Each player controls his or her ball and passes it to the feeder in the circle on the same side of the field. This player controls and turns with the ball, dribbles toward the goal, and shoots on goal from outside the 18-yard line. The shooters go to the end of the appropriate lines and the passers become the center circle players.

VARIATIONS: 1. Add a defender to create a one vs. one situation with the shooter.
2. Have the passer overlap the wing, creating a two vs. one situation.

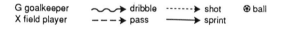

G goalkeeper	∿∿➤ dribble	┈┈┈➤ shot	⊕ ball
X field player	─ ─➤ pass	──➤ sprint	

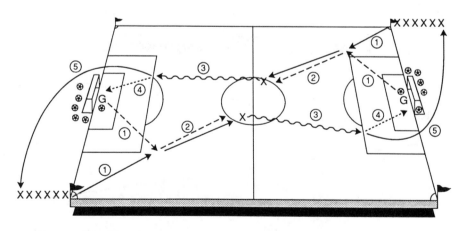

CONTRIBUTOR: Efrain Borja, Boys' Assistant Coach, Elizabeth High School, Elizabeth, New Jersey

Attacking Skills

FOCUS	AREA	PERSONNEL	EQUIPMENT
Passing	Two 10 × 10	5 players	1 ball
Receiving¯	grids		6 cones
Possession			2 vests

FORMATION: There are three attackers and two defenders. The defenders wear vests. Two attackers, one with a ball, and one defender are in a 10 × 10 yard grid. The remaining attacker and defender are in an adjacent 10 × 10 yard grid.

PROCEDURE: A1 and A2 control the ball against D1 within their grid. A3 makes runs to get free from D2 in the other grid to receive a pass from A1 or A2. The player who passes the ball into the other grid follows the pass and plays two vs. one in that grid. The remaining player is now one vs. one in the grid and moves to get free to receive a pass.

VARIATION: Enlarge the grids and increase the number of players.
- A. Three vs. two and two vs. two
- B. Four vs. three and three vs. three

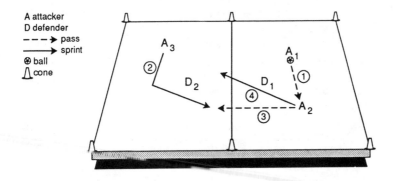

A attacker
D defender
- - - → pass
——→ sprint
⊕ ball
⋀ cone

CONTRIBUTOR: Loren E. Kline, Men's Coach, University of Delaware, Newark, Delaware

Bahia

FOCUS	AREA	PERSONNEL	EQUIPMENT
Attack	Penalty area	20+	10 balls
Shooting	and adjacent		1 goal
Goalkeeping	area		
Crossing			
Heading			

FORMATION: The balls are evenly divided in two areas outside both sides of the penalty area near the touchline with two serving players in each area (X1 and X5). Goalkeepers take turns in the goal; the goalkeepers not in the goal serve as retrievers. Players are in three vertical lines (X2, X3, and X4). Two lines (X2 and X4) are 12 yards from the goal on both sides of goal area. One line (X3) is in the middle of the 18-yard line.

PROCEDURE: X1 dribbles to the end line and crosses the ball to the middle or to the near or far post. X2, X3, and X4 time their runs so that X2 meets the ball between the 12-yard and the 6-yard area, or X3 meets the ball at the far post, or X4 meets the ball at the near post. After meeting the ball the player shoots on the goal. Once done, players switch to new lines. X5 then repeats the drill from the left side with X4, X3, and X2 reversing runs. After several serves, players on the flanks switch with the striking players.

VARIATION: Add defenders.

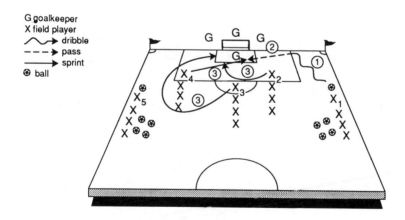

CONTRIBUTOR: C. Cliff McCrath, Men's Coach, Seattle Pacific University, Seattle, Washington

Beat That Pass

FOCUS	AREA	PERSONNEL	EQUIPMENT
Fitness	1/2 field or	8 players	1 ball
Passing	less		1 cone

FORMATION: Players X1 through X6 form a line. A cone is placed 10 to 20 yards in front of the line (the distance depends on how much sprinting is desired and the distance that the ball is being kicked). X8 is about 40 yards from the beginning of the line and X7 is stationed near the cone.

PROCEDURE: X1 kicks the ball forward past X8, if possible. X1 then sprints around the cone and back to the beginning of the line. Meanwhile X8, who can be a field player or a goalkeeper, retrieves the ball and attempts to hit X1 with it or throws it to X7 to hit X1 before X1 returns to the beginning of the line. Players can keep score if they wish. The sprinter scores 1 point for getting back to the start without being hit; the retrievers score 1 point if they hit the sprinter before he or she returns to the beginning of the line. After the sequence is completed X1 goes to the back of the line and X2 passes the ball to X8.

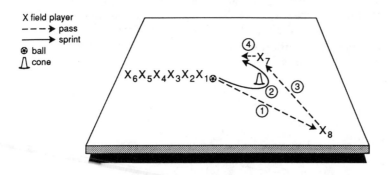

CONTRIBUTOR: Jay Miller, Men's Coach, University of South Florida, Tampa, Florida

Beat Your Opponent

FOCUS	AREA	PERSONNEL	EQUIPMENT
Fitness	1/2 field	9 players	1 ball
Dribbling			1 goal
Shooting			

FORMATION: Two lines—one with four attackers and one with four defenders—are outside opposite goalposts facing midfield. A goalkeeper with a ball is in the goal.

PROCEDURE: The goalkeeper punts or throws the ball toward the center circle. One attacker and one defender sprint to the ball. The first player to reach the ball must dribble it back toward the goalkeeper while the other player attempts to steal the ball. The attacker must get off a shot by the 18-yard line, whereas the defender must dribble the ball back to the goalkeeper.

VARIATIONS:
1. Set up different situations; e.g., two vs. one, two vs. two, three vs. two, up to four vs. four.
2. As the number of players increases permit two or three passes.

A attacker
D defender
G goalkeeper
〜〜➤ dribble
− − −➤ pass
———➤ sprint
⊛ ball

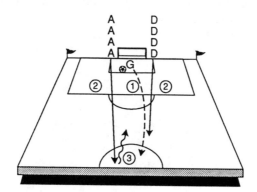

CONTRIBUTOR: Daniel Coombs, Boys' Coach, Loyola Academy, Wilmette, Illinois

Bogies in the Sky

FOCUS	AREA	PERSONNEL	EQUIPMENT
Attack	1/2 field	Whole team	6 balls
Defense			1 goal

FORMATION: The team is divided into three groups of equal numbers. A group of attackers is by one goalpost, a group of defenders is by the other goalpost, and a group of midfielders is at midfield. A supply of balls is at midfield. A goalkeeper is in the goal.

PROCEDURE: A midfielder passes a ball to an attacker, who is sprinting out at an angle toward the 18-yard line. A defender moves out to cover the attacker. The midfielder follows the pass to give the attacker a passing option. The attacker, after looking to determine the defender's position, decides whether to turn and take on the defender or pass to the midfielder. If the ball is passed, an additional defender and midfielder join the drill for each pass made. Play continues until an attack is finished with a shot on goal or the ball is intercepted. When play is complete attackers, defenders, and midfielders go to the end of the line from which they started.

VARIATION: Use two defenders. The first one moves out at the same time as the attacker, and the second defender sprints out when the attacker receives the ball.

A attacker
D defender
G goalkeeper
M midfielder
– – –▶ pass
——▶ sprint
⊕ ball

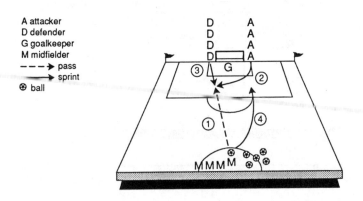

CONTRIBUTOR: Anson Dorrance, Women's Coach, University of North Carolina, Chapel Hill, North Carolina

Build Up— Numbers Down

FOCUS	AREA	PERSONNEL	EQUIPMENT
Attack	20 × 30 yards	8 players	1 ball
Transition			4 cones
			4 vests

FORMATION: There are two teams of four players each. One team wears vests. Two cones, 1 yard apart, mark the goals at each end of the 20 × 30 yard grid.

PROCEDURE: Play starts with one player from each team going one vs. one attempting to score. Each time a goal is scored the team not scoring adds a player until there is a four vs. four setup. At this point, each time a goal is scored the team scoring takes away a player. Play ends when one team gets all of its players off the field..

Scoring system: 1 point—goal with numerical advantage
2 points—goal with numbers even
3 points—goal with numbers down
5 points—first team to get all players off

Example:

Players/Teams		Scoring	
A B	Scoring team	A	B
1 vs. 1	A	2	0
1 vs. 2	B	2	1
2 vs. 2	B	2	3
3 vs. 2	B	2	6
4 vs. 2	A	3	6
4 vs. 3	A	4	6
4 vs. 4	A	6	6
3 vs. 4	B	6	7
3 vs. 3	A	8	6
2 vs. 3	A	11	7
1 vs. 3	B	11	8
1 vs. 2	A	14	8
Game over	A wins (bonus)	19	8

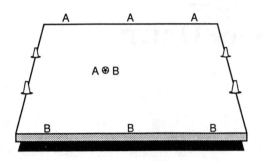

CONTRIBUTOR: Jack Poland, Women's Coach, University of North Carolina, Greensboro, North Carolina

Building Defensive Pressure

FOCUS	AREA	PERSONNEL	EQUIPMENT
Defense	Penalty area	13 players	1 ball
Attack			1 goal

FORMATION: Initial play is two vs. one. Twelve players, in four groups of three players each, are randomly positioned within the penalty area. One player has a ball. A goalkeeper is in the goal.

PROCEDURE: Each group plays two vs. one keep-away for 2 minutes. Play then changes to groups alternately playing five vs. two (two attackers play continuously) with the emphasis on the second defender covering the pressuring defender and helping prevent the two defenders from being "split." Finally, play eight vs. four with a goalkeeper. Eight attackers play one touch and must complete 10 consecutive passes before taking a shot on goal. Any intercepted passes are immediately passed to the goalkeeper.

VARIATION: Follow the same procedure with the emphasis on attacking.

A attacker
D defender
G goalkeeper
⊕ ball

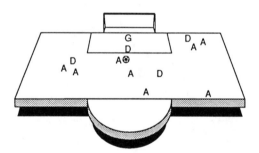

CONTRIBUTOR: J. Kevin Denson, Boys' Coach, Kempsville High School, Virginia Beach, Virginia

Central Zone Play

FOCUS	AREA	PERSONNEL	EQUIPMENT
Natural play	60 × 44 yards	12 players	1 ball
Fitness			2 goals
Fun			5 vests

FORMATION: A 60 × 44 yard area is divided into three zones of 20 yards each with a regulation goal on each end line. Two groups, each with five players and a goalkeeper, are positioned within the area as follows: a goalkeeper in each goal, two defenders vs. one attacker in each end zone, and two vs. two in the center zone. One team wears vests.

PROCEDURE: Play is started with a drop ball in the center zone. Play continues as in a regulation game. Each team attempts to shoot on goal as soon as possible. During play, players can move forward one zone to attack but cannot move back to defend beyond the zone in which they started.

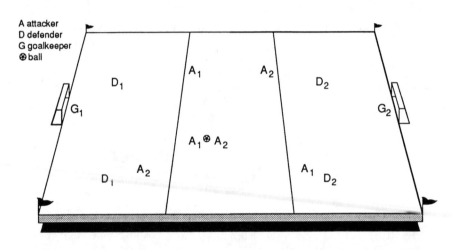

CONTRIBUTOR: Jack Mackenzie, Men's Coach, Quincy College, Quincy, Illinois

Change of Direction

FOCUS	**AREA**	**PERSONNEL**	**EQUIPMENT**
Receiving	10 × 20 yards	3 players	2 balls
Turning			
Passing			

FORMATION: Three players are in a straight line within a 10 × 20 yard grid—two outside players, each with a ball, face a player in the middle.

PROCEDURE: X1 makes a ground pass to X3, who returns a one-touch pass to X1. Following the return pass, X3 turns quickly to receive a pass from X2, who has timed the pass so that X3 receives it on the turn. X3 makes a one-touch return pass to X2 and turns again for the next pass from X1. Play continues for 30 to 60 seconds, after which the players rotate positions.

VARIATIONS:
1. The middle player controls the ball with one foot and passes it with the other.
2. Outside players throw or kick balls to the middle player at different angles.
3. Using one ball, X1 passes the ball to X3, who controls it, turns with it, and passes it to X2, who one touches it back to X3, and so on.
4. Put a passive defender on the middle player.

X field player
− − −▶ pass
⊛ ball

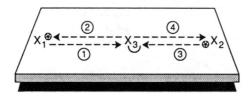

CONTRIBUTOR: Robert Dubiel, Boys' Coach, Northampton High School, Northampton, Massachusetts

Checking

FOCUS	AREA	PERSONNEL	EQUIPMENT
Movement with/without the ball Passing Receiving Attack Defense	40 × 20 yards	4 players	1 ball

FORMATION: One attacker and one defender are in the middle of a 40 × 20 yard grid. Two other players, X1 and X2, are outside opposite ends of the grid. X1 has a ball.

PROCEDURE: The attacker starts the drill by moving (checking) toward the defender and then making a quick diagonal run into open space. X1 must pass the ball as soon as the attacker makes the run. The defender challenges the attacker. The drill is repeated five times; then the attacker and defender rotate positions and X2 passes the ball to the attacker.

VARIATIONS:
1. The attacker controls the pass and goes one vs. one with the defender in an attempt to pass the ball to X2.
2. Add a goal and a goalkeeper; the attacker tries to beat the defender and shoot on goal.

A attacker
D defender
X field player
– – –► pass
———► sprint
⊕ ball

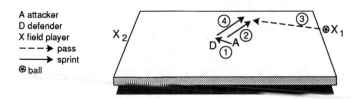

CONTRIBUTOR: Nick Mykulak, Men's Coach, Stevens Tech, Hoboken, New Jersey

Chip-Trap-Pass-Shot

FOCUS	AREA	PERSONNEL	EQUIPMENT
Shooting	Penalty area	Full team	5 balls
Passing			1 goal
Control			

FORMATION: The team is divided into three lines of equal numbers. Line A is on the end line at one corner of the penalty area. Each player in line A has a ball. Line B is on the opposite corner end line. Line C is at the top of the penalty area arc. A goalkeeper is in the goal.

PROCEDURE: The first player in line A chips a ball across the penalty area to the first player in line B. This player controls and passes the ball to the top of the penalty area for the first player in line C to shoot on goal. Following the shot on goal, the shooter retrieves the ball and goes to the end of line A, the passer from line A rotates to the end of line B, and the passer from line B rotates to the end of line C.

VARIATION: Make all passes and shots one-touch.

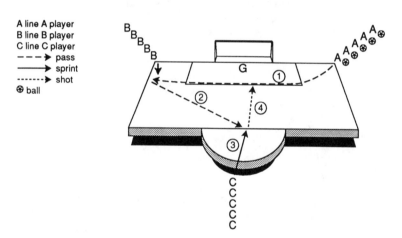

A line A player
B line B player
C line C player
– – –► pass
——► sprint
······► shot
⊛ ball

CONTRIBUTOR: Richard G. Zawacki, Boys' Coach, Don Bosco Prep, Ramsey, New Jersey

Commit to the Ball

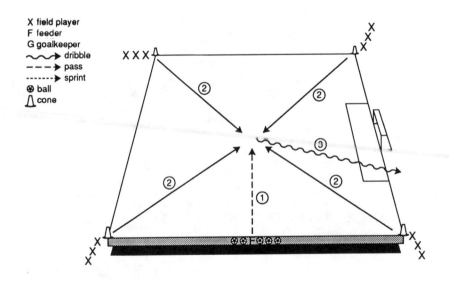

FOCUS	AREA	PERSONNEL	EQUIPMENT
Commitment Movement 　with/with- 　out the ball	30 × 30 yards	12 players 1 feeder	5 balls 4 cones 1 goal

FORMATION: Three players are lined up behind each of four cones placed at each corner of a 30 × 30 yard area. A feeder with a supply of balls is just outside the area.

PROCEDURE: The feeder begins the drill with a pass into the middle of the area. As soon as the ball is touched, the first player in each line sprints to the ball. The first player to reach the ball calls off the other players, who then move into support positions as the player with the ball dribbles toward the goal. Play ends when the ball is dribbled out of the area. After each play, the players rotate counterclockwise to the end of another line and play continues with another pass.

VARIATIONS: 1. Use a goal and end each play with a shot on goal from the 18-yard line.
2. Add two defenders.

X field player
F feeder
G goalkeeper
~~~► dribble
– – –► pass
······► sprint
⊕ ball
∆ cone

CONTRIBUTOR: Margie Shade, Women's Coach, Ohio Wesleyan University, Delaware, Ohio

Conditioning to Shoot

FOCUS	AREA	PERSONNEL	EQUIPMENT
Shooting	Penalty area	10+ players	8 balls
Fitness			2 cones
Goalkeeping			1 goal

FORMATION: There are eight feeders, each with a ball. Two feeders are at each of four locations outside the penalty area. A 9th player, the attacker, starts outside and between two cones placed 10 yards outside the penalty area in line with the goalpost. The 10th player is the goalkeeper. Other players spread out behind the goal and serve as retrievers.

PROCEDURE: The attacker has 60 seconds to get off eight shots at the goal. All shots will be one touched from the semicircle arc of the penalty area. After each shot, the attacker must sprint around one of the cones and be ready for the next pass in the semicircle arc. F1 passes a ball to the arc, then F2, and so on until all eight shots have been taken; then players rotate positions.

VARIATIONS:
1. Feeders use push passes on the ground.
2. Feeders chip balls to the attacker.
3. Feeders hit bouncing balls to the attacker.

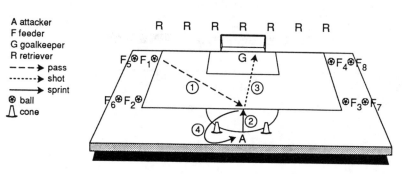

A attacker
F feeder
G goalkeeper
R retriever
- - - ➤ pass
------➤ shot
———➤ sprint
⊛ ball
⌂ cone

CONTRIBUTOR: Michael C. Mooney, Men's Coach, SUNY College at Geneseo, Geneseo, New York

Consecutive Passes

FOCUS	AREA	PERSONNEL	EQUIPMENT
Passing	1/2 field	12 players	1 ball
Defense			1 goal
Fitness			6 vests

FORMATION: Two teams, each with six players, occupy half the soccer field. One team wears vests. One team has a soccer ball.

PROCEDURE: The team in possession of the ball attempts to complete 10 consecutive passes. A new count starts whenever ball possession changes. The first team to complete 10 consecutive passes wins.

VARIATIONS: 1. Restrict individual control to one or two touches.
2. Restrict players to using only the left or the right foot.

A attacker
D defender
– – –> pass
———> sprint
⊕ ball

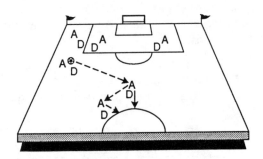

CONTRIBUTOR: Schellas Hyndman, Men's Coach, Southern Methodist University, Dallas, Texas

Control-Switch

FOCUS	AREA	PERSONNEL	EQUIPMENT
Passing	35 × 15 yards	12 players	4 balls
Switching		1 coach	8 cones
Fitness			3 sets of
			4 vests

FORMATION: Two grids, each 15 × 15 yards and marked by cones, are 5 yards apart. Four attacking players are in each grid and four defenders are in the neutral zone. The players on each team wear different colored vests. A coach stands outside the area between the grids with four balls.

PROCEDURE: The coach plays a ball into grid A. The attacking players in that grid attempt to make five consecutive passes under the pressure of two defenders from the neutral zone. After the fifth pass the ball should be passed to grid B. If the ball is passed successfully, the two defensive players still in the neutral zones move to grid B and the first pair of defenders return to the neutral zone. If five passes are not made or the switch pass is not successful the players in grid A become defenders, following the procedure just described. The coach plays another ball into grid B. The middle players can play errant passes.

VARIATIONS: 1. Change the number of players.
2. Use one- and two-touch restrictions.
3. Change the size of the grids and the distance between grids.

A attacker   – – – ▸ pass
D defender   ⎯⎯▸ sprint
C coach   ⊕ ball
N neutral zone player   ⛛ cone

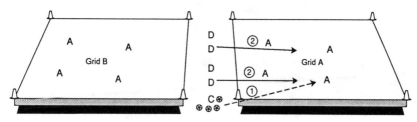

CONTRIBUTOR: Dr. Jay Martin, Men's Coach, Ohio Wesleyan University, Delaware, Ohio

Controlling in the Circle

FOCUS	AREA	PERSONNEL	EQUIPMENT
Control	Center circle	12 players	4 balls
Passing			
Fitness			

FORMATION: There are three groups of four players each. Two groups are spread around the perimeter of the center circle with a ball for every other player. The third group is the working group inside the circle.

PROCEDURE: Depending on the controlling technique being emphasized, the feeders pass or toss balls to players inside the circle (pass to feet; toss to thigh, chest, or head). Field players move within the circle, call and show for the ball from the feeder, receive and control it, and pass it to another feeder who does not have a ball. Continue for 3 minutes, after which one outside group switches with the inside group.

VARIATIONS: 1. Increase the number of players and the size of the playing area.
2. Add defenders within the circle. The feeders must call "turn" or "man on" before passing to field players.
3. Use two touch or, if man on, one touch.

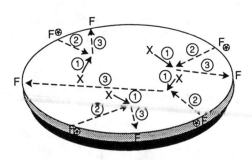

CONTRIBUTOR: Karen Stanley, Women's Coach, Seattle Pacific University, Seattle, Washington

Corner Kick

FOCUS	AREA	PERSONNEL	EQUIPMENT
Attack	Penalty area	7 players	5 balls
Clearing	and adjacent		1 goal
	area		

FORMATION: An attacker, A1, with five balls is at one corner of the field. Three attackers, A2, A3, and A4, line up shoulder-to-shoulder on the 18-yard line. Two attackers, A5 and A6, are outside the penalty area on the side of the field opposite A1. A goalkeeper is in the goal.

PROCEDURE: Before serving a ball into the goal area, A1 signals the start of the drill by lowering one hand on the approach to the ball. At this signal A2 makes a run around A3 and A4 to the far post, A3 makes a run around A4 to the center of the goal area, A4 makes a diagonal run to the near post, A5 makes a run around A6 to the 18-yard line, and A6 delays a run to the area outside the far post. A first-time shot on goal is attempted by the player who contacts the ball.

VARIATION: Add defenders to mark each attacker.

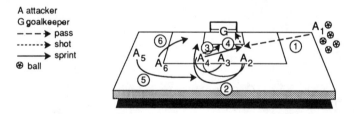

```
A attacker
G goalkeeper
– – –➤ pass
·······➤ shot
———➤ sprint
⊕ ball
```

CONTRIBUTOR: Joe Collins, Girls' Coach, Indian Hills High School, Oakland, New Jersey

Counter Drill

FOCUS	AREA	PERSONNEL	EQUIPMENT
Attack	75 × 35 yards	8 players	7 balls
Fitness			2 goals

FORMATION: Eight players are divided into four teams of two players each. Two teams are in the middle, one team is off the field, and one team serves as goalkeepers. One ball is on the field and three balls are in each goal easily accessible to each goalkeeper.

PROCEDURE: The two teams on the field play two vs. two until someone scores. The goalkeepers then come on the field to challenge the winners, the off-field team becomes the goalkeepers, and the losers become the off-field team. Continue this rotation.

VARIATIONS: 1. Shorten the field.
2. Play three vs. three.

A attacker
D defender
G goalkeeper
O off-field player
⊛ ball

CONTRIBUTOR: Lenny Long, Men's Coach, Lock Haven University, Lock Haven, Pennsylvania

Create Space

FOCUS	AREA	PERSONNEL	EQUIPMENT
Passing	10 × 10 yards	3 players	1 ball
Support			

FORMATION: Three players, one with a ball, are positioned at different corners of a 10 × 10 yard grid.

PROCEDURE: X1 passes across the grid to X2. After the pass, X1 moves to a support position (the unoccupied corner of the grid). This gives X2 two passing options. X2 passes to either corner player, checks away in the opposite direction, and moves back to his or her original position (no diagonal runs).

VARIATIONS: 1. Limit the number of touches.
2. Add a defender.

X field player
- - -► pass
———► sprint
⊕ ball

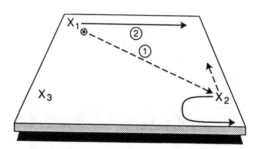

CONTRIBUTOR: Brian Chafin, Men's Coach, Centre College, Danville, Kentucky

Crosses and Shots

FOCUS	AREA	PERSONNEL	EQUIPMENT
Shooting	1/3 field	8 players	2 balls
Fun			1 goal

FORMATION: Two groups, X and Y, of four players each are positioned within the attacking third of the field as shown in the diagram. There are two crossers and two shooters in each group. One crosser in each group has a ball.

PROCEDURE: The X player with the ball passes to the nearest teammate, sprints toward the penalty area, receives a through pass, and crosses to either of the shooters, who have made runs toward the near and far posts. The groups cross and shoot alternately. The first group to score three goals wins; then the groups change sides and the shooters become crossers.

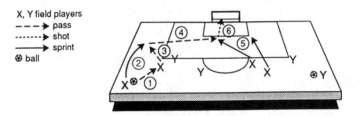

X, Y field players
- - - ▶ pass
······▶ shot
——▶ sprint
⊛ ball

CONTRIBUTOR: Alan Kirkup, Women's Coach, Southern Methodist University, Dallas, Texas

Crossing Exercise

FOCUS	AREA	PERSONNEL	EQUIPMENT
Crossing	1/2 field	12 players	4 balls
Fitness		1 feeder	4 cones
Defense			1 goal

FORMATION: Three lines, X, Y, and Z, with four players each are at midfield as shown in the diagram. A feeder with four balls stands near the midfield sideline. Four cones form an alley 10 yards inside one sideline.

PROCEDURE: The feeder passes a ball to Y, who dribbles down the alley and, after passing the last cone, crosses the ball to the area between the penalty mark and the goal area. X and Z make bent runs toward the near and far posts, respectively. The player receiving the cross controls it and returns it to the feeder. Three new players continue the drill. After each cross, the players go to the end of the next line, rotating counterclockwise.

VARIATIONS: 1. Add a defender to mark X or Z.
2. Add two defenders.

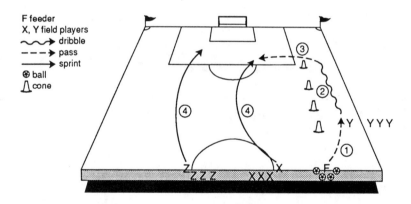

F feeder
X, Y field players
〜〜➤ dribble
− − −➤ pass
──➤ sprint
⊕ ball
⨅ cone

CONTRIBUTOR: David Springer, Boys' Coach, Binghamton High School, Binghamton, New York

29

Defensive Heading

FOCUS	AREA	PERSONNEL	EQUIPMENT
Fitness	1/3 field	8 players	8 balls
		2 feeders	1 goal

FORMATION: Ten players are positioned as follows:

1. Two attackers outside each side of the penalty area
2. Two defenders inside each side of the penalty area
3. A feeder on each sideline about 30 yards from the end-line; each feeder has four balls

PROCEDURE: Each feeder serves balls alternately to the attackers and defenders on the same side of the field. The two attackers in each group try to head the ball on goal whereas the two defenders work on marking and clearing balls out of the area.

A attacker
D defender
F feeder
− − −▸ pass
⊛ ball

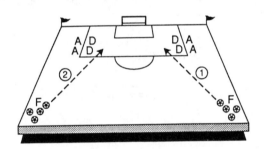

CONTRIBUTOR: Dave Masur, Men's Coach, Montclair State College, Upper Montclair, New Jersey

Delay and Recover

FOCUS	AREA	PERSONNEL	EQUIPMENT
Defense Commu- nication	15 × 30 yards	4 players	1 ball

FORMATION: Formation: Two attackers, A1 and A2, are positioned within a 15 × 30 yard grid. A defender with a ball, D1, is on the end line nearest the attackers. A second defender, D2, is within the grid between the attackers and the opposite end line.

PROCEDURE: D1 passes to A1. D1 counts slowly to three while D2 moves to delay A1 from getting to the opposite end line. After the count of three, D1 recovers goalside of everyone to cover and support D2. A1 may pass to A2 to progress to the end of the grid. The object of the drill is for the defenders to delay for 10 seconds and the attackers to attempt to get the ball to the opposite end line.

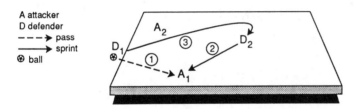

A attacker
D defender
- - -▶ pass
——▶ sprint
⊕ ball

CONTRIBUTOR: Fred Schmalz, Men's Coach, University of Evansville, Evansville, Indiana

Dribble and Pass

FOCUS	AREA	PERSONNEL	EQUIPMENT
Fitness	Full field	14 players	1 ball for each
Passing		2 feeders	player
Crossing			2 goals
Shooting			

FORMATION: Players are divided into two groups. Each group forms a vertical line at a corner of each end line diagonally opposite the other group. Each player has a ball. A feeder for each group is at midfield. A goalkeeper is in each goal.

PROCEDURE: The first player in each line begins the drill by pushing the ball forward and dribbling at top speed toward midfield. Before reaching midfield the dribblers make a wall pass to the feeders, get the ball back, and dribble on to an area outside the penalty area where they make a cross to the goalkeepers. They go behind the goal, receive the ball back from the goalkeepers, and go to the end of the opposite line.

VARIATION: After getting the ball back from the feeder, the dribblers cut in toward the goal and shoot.

F feeder
G goalkeeper
X field player
〜〜➤ dribble
− − −➤ pass
······➤ shot
———➤ sprint
⊕ ball

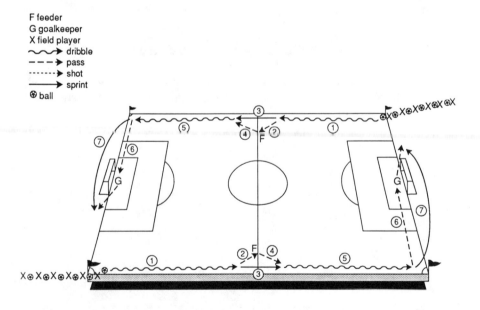

CONTRIBUTOR: Jeff Tipping, Men's Coach, Muhlenberg College, Allentown, Pennsylvania

Dry Run

FOCUS	AREA	PERSONNEL	EQUIPMENT
Position play	Full field	22 players	1 ball
Movement			2 goals
with/without			10 vests
the ball			

FORMATION: Two full teams are positioned in a full field. One team wears vests. A goalkeeper is in each goal. One of the goalkeepers has a ball.

PROCEDURE: The goalkeeper distributes the ball to a fullback. The ball is advanced by two-touch play from the defensive third of the field to the attacking third. Play ends with a shot on goal. The team without the ball offers passive (20%) defense, permitting the passing and the shot on goal. After the shot, play continues in the reverse direction with the teams changing roles.

VARIATION: Increase defensive pressure: 50%, 75%, 100%.

A attacker
D defender
G goalkeeper
– – –➤ pass
------➤ shot
——➤ sprint
⊕ ball

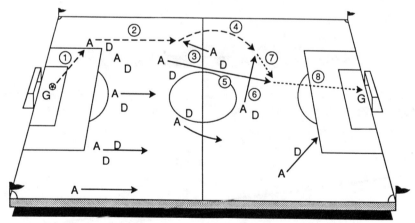

CONTRIBUTOR: Gene Chyzowych, Boys' Coach, Columbia High School, Maplewood, New Jersey

Five-Spot Keeper

FOCUS	AREA	PERSONNEL	EQUIPMENT
Goalkeeping	1/2 field	7 players	15 balls
Passing			1 goal
Shooting			

FORMATION: X1 and X2 are in opposite corners. X3 and X4 are near midfield on opposite sidelines. X5 is in the center about 30 yards from the goal. Each player has three balls. A goalkeeper is in the goal with a second goalkeeper behind the goal.

PROCEDURE: X1 starts with a cross on goal, followed by X2 with a cross, X3 with a long shot, X4 with a long shot, and X5 with any type of shot on goal. The next person kicks as soon as the goalkeeper clears or catches the ball. After the goalkeeper goes through two or three rotations, switch goalkeepers and have players rotate positions.

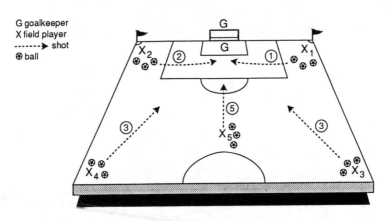

G goalkeeper
X field player
------> shot
⊕ ball

CONTRIBUTOR: Roger Essmann, Boys' Coach, Earlville High School, Earlville, Illinois

Five vs. Five Shooting

FOCUS	AREA	PERSONNEL	EQUIPMENT
Shooting	25 × 40 yards	17 players	5 balls
Goalkeeping			2 goals
			15 vests

FORMATION: There are three teams of five players each. Each team wears different colored vests. Two of the teams are positioned in opposite halves of a 20 × 40 yard area. The players on the third team are located outside the area and serve as retrievers. A player on one of the field teams has a ball. A goalkeeper is in each goal. Two balls are behind each goal.

PROCEDURE: The two teams on the field play five vs. five for 45-minute periods. The objective is to take as many good shots on goal as possible during each period. The goalkeepers and retrievers help keep action continuous by getting a ball back in play after each shot or out-of-bounds play. One point is awarded for each shot on goal, 2 points for each goal, and 5 points for each goal made after a give and go. The winning team takes on the third team after the first period. In succeeding periods, the team that has played two shifts gets a rest.

VARIATIONS: 1. Set up your own point system.
2. Use a one- or two-touch restriction.
3. Use one or two target players for shooters.

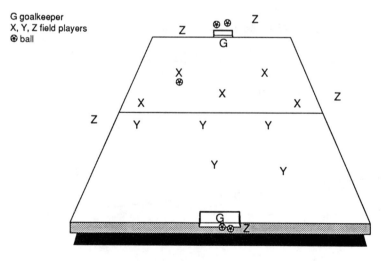

G goalkeeper
X, Y, Z field players
⊕ ball

CONTRIBUTOR: Karen Lombardo, Women's Coach, Florissant Valley Community College, St. Louis, Missouri

Five vs. Three vs. One

FOCUS	AREA	PERSONNEL	EQUIPMENT
Movement with/without the ball Defense Control	20 × 20 yards	8 players	1 ball 4 cones 3 vests

FORMATION: Three attackers, one with a ball, and one defender (D1) are inside a 20 × 20 yard grid, which is marked by four cones. Four defenders are spread around the perimeter of the grid. The attackers wear vests.

PROCEDURE: Play is three vs. one within the grid. The outside defenders cannot assist the middle defender. Whenever the attackers lose possession of the ball, they are forced to defend five vs. three with D1 maintaining a central support position. Players rotate after a designated period.

A attacker
D defender
 ball
cone

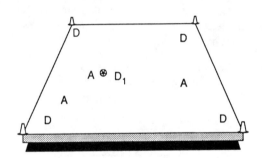

CONTRIBUTOR: Joe Waldron, Assistant Men's Coach, University of Evansville, Evansville, Indiana

Five vs. Two Plus One

FOCUS	AREA	PERSONNEL	EQUIPMENT
Passing	Center circle	8 players	1 ball
Support			6 vests
Defense			

FORMATION: Five attackers, one with a ball, are spread around the perimeter of the center circle. Two defenders and one attacker are inside the circle. The attackers wear vests.

PROCEDURE: The drill starts with a five vs. two keep-away emphasizing passing and support. A target player is added within the circle to set up a five vs. two plus one keep-away. The target player has a one-touch restriction and is used to support the attackers and change the point of attack.

VARIATION: Add a third defender and emphasize defensive organization.

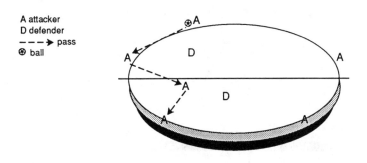

A attacker
D defender
‑ ‑ ‑▶ pass
⊛ ball

CONTRIBUTOR: Dr. Tom Martin, Men's Coach, James Madison University, Harrisonburg, Virginia

Flank Crossing

FOCUS	AREA	PERSONNEL	EQUIPMENT
Attack	1/3 field	8 players	2 balls
Defense		2 feeders	1 goal

FORMATION: Five attackers are spread outside the penalty area. Two defenders are within the goal area and a goalkeeper is in the goal. Two feeders each have a ball. Each feeder is about 10 yards away from a wide attacker on opposite sides of the field.

PROCEDURE: The feeder positioned near A1 passes the ball forward on the flank to A1, who collects the ball and dribbles down the flank. While A1 is dribbling, A2, A3, and A4 move to the far post, near post, and penalty mark, respectively. Each defender must mark one attacker, leaving one attacker free for A1 to locate. After dribbling down the flank, A1 looks up, locates the free player, and crosses the ball to that player, who shoots on goal first time. After each attack is finished, the players return to their initial positions and play continues, alternating the feeder and flank player (A1 or A5) on each side of the field.

A attacker
D defender
F feeder
G goalkeeper
〜〜➤ dribble
− − −➤ pass
······➤ shot
──➤ sprint
⊕ ball

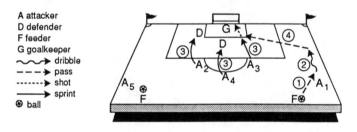

CONTRIBUTOR: Buddy Hayford, Boys' Coach, Wilmington High School, Wilmington, Vermont

Four-Corner Finishing

FOCUS	AREA	PERSONNEL	EQUIPMENT
Shooting	40 × 40 yards	16 players	10 balls
Passing			4 goals
Goalkeeping			

FORMATION: Each of four portable goals is on each sideline of a 40 × 40 yard grid. A goalkeeper is in each goal. Three players line up at the right post of each goal facing the opposite goal. Each player except the first player in lines A and B has a ball. A coach stands in the middle of the grid.

PROCEDURE: X1 and X3 sprint to the middle of the grid, bend around the coach, show to X2 and X4 respectively, receive a pass from those players, and shoot on goals C and D respectively. Following each shot, the shooter sprints to retrieve the ball and joins the end of the line at the goal at which the shot was taken. X2 and X4 continue in the same manner, and this rotation is followed throughout the drill. No shot may be taken within 10 yards of the goal.

VARIATIONS: 1. Players take two- or one-touch shots.
2. Vary the types of passes to encourage volley, side volley, or half volley shots.
3. Move the goals closer and have passers take throwins to encourage head shots.

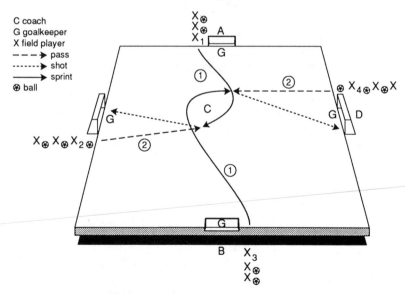

C coach
G goalkeeper
X field player
– – –▶ pass
······▶ shot
——▶ sprint
⊕ ball

CONTRIBUTOR: Jeff Vagell, Women's Assistant Coach, Wesleyan University, Middletown, Connecticut

Four-Corner Shoot

FOCUS	AREA	PERSONNEL	EQUIPMENT
Shooting	30-yard area in	16 players	5 balls
Goalkeeping	front of goal		1 goal
Passing			

FORMATION: Players form five lines of three players each as indicated in the diagram. A goalkeeper is in the goal. Balls are at line A—the starting line.

PROCEDURE: The first player in line A (starting line) passes to the first player in line B, who passes to line C, who passes to line D, who passes to the first player in line E, the shooting line. This player shoots first time. Players sprint to the end of the line to which they passed the ball. The shooter sprints to the end of the starting line.

VARIATIONS: 1. The drill can be done from either side.
2. Adjust the angle and distance of the shot.
3. Limit players to one touch in passing.

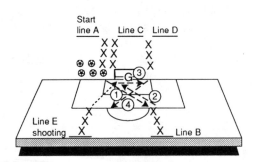

CONTRIBUTOR: Ronald W. Shewcraft, Men's Coach, North Adams State College, North Adams, Massachusetts

Four Corners

FOCUS	AREA	PERSONNEL	EQUIPMENT
Aggressiveness	30 × 30 yards	4 players	1 ball
Fitness		1 feeder	

FORMATION: One player is at each corner of a 30 × 30 yard grid. A feeder with one ball is located just outside the grid.

PROCEDURE: The feeder kicks a ball into the center of the grid and calls "play." All the players sprint to the ball. The first player to reach the ball must keep possession from the other players for 5 seconds before passing the ball back to the feeder. Likewise, any player taking the ball away from the player with possession must hold the ball for 5 seconds before the drill is completed.

VARIATIONS: 1. Vary the types of passes.
2. Create two vs. two or three vs. one situations and require 10 passes for a team to finish the drill.

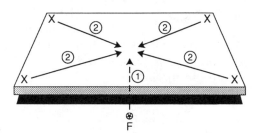

CONTRIBUTOR: George D. Danner, Boys' Coach, Griffin High School, Griffin, Georgia

Four Lines
Toward the Cone

FOCUS	AREA	PERSONNEL	EQUIPMENT
Dribbling	20 × 20 yards	8 players	4 balls
Shielding			1 cone

FORMATION: Two players are in each of four lines facing a cone in the center of the grid. The first player in each line has a ball.

PROCEDURE: The players dribble toward the cone simultaneously. When they reach the cone they turn to the right, move to the next line, and give up the ball to the person waiting in that line to repeat the movement. The drill is run with the following six basic movement variations. Each movement is practiced simultaneously by all players for 2 to 3 minutes.

VARIATIONS:
1. Cut the ball with the inside of the right foot.
2. Cut the ball with the inside of the left foot.
3. Cut the ball with the outside of the right foot.
4. Cut the ball with the outside of the left foot.
5. Pull the ball back with the sole of the right foot.
6. Pull the ball back with the sole of the left foot and turn to the left.

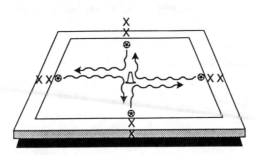

X field player
dribble
⊗ ball
⌂ cone

CONTRIBUTOR: Jim Braun, Boys' Coach, Naperville Central High School, Naperville, Illinois

Four Square Triangles

FOCUS	AREA	PERSONNEL	EQUIPMENT
Movement with/without the ball	10 × 20 yards	4 players	1 ball
			4 cones
Passing			
Fitness			

FORMATION: Four cones mark the corners of a 10 × 20 yard grid. Three attackers stand alongside any three cones. A defender is in the middle. One attacker has a ball.

PROCEDURE: Passes must be within the grid. A1 passes to A2 or A3. After the first pass, D begins pressuring the ball. The player receiving the pass must be able to see an open player directly to the left or right. Therefore, the offensive player not making or receiving the pass must run to the open cone. Play continues until D intercepts a pass, a bad pass is made, or an attacker forgets to move to an open cone. When one of these situations occurs, D changes places with the offending attacker.

VARIATIONS: 1. Players change places after 10 successful passes.
2. Set a time limit, such as 5 minutes.

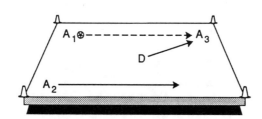

CONTRIBUTOR: Jeffrey L. Bickley, Marion, Ohio

Four vs. Four vs. Four

FOCUS	AREA	PERSONNEL	EQUIPMENT
Transition	Full field	14 players	1 ball
Midfield play			4 cones
			2 goals
			8 vests

FORMATION: Three groups of four players each are on the field. Two of the teams, X and Z, start as defenders at opposite ends of the field. The third team, Y, with a ball, starts as attackers from the neutral zone (10 yards either side of midfield), which is marked by cones. A goalkeeper is in each goal.

PROCEDURE: Team Y attacks team Z. When Z wins the ball or gives up a goal, they attack Y toward midfield. When they penetrate with possession into the neutral zone they are free and now attack team X. Teams cannot follow an attacking team into the neutral zone. Play continues in this fashion with two teams changing roles on each goal or loss of possession.

VARIATIONS: 1. Add two chasers in the neutral zone to play keep-away from the attacking team.
2. Play two touch through the neutral zone.
3. Play one touch through the neutral zone.

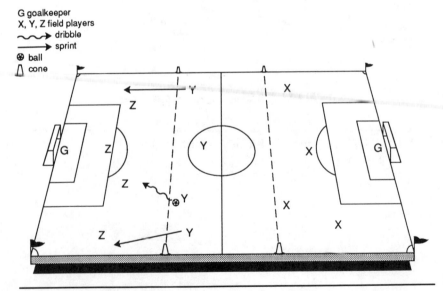

G goalkeeper
X, Y, Z field players
⌁⟶ dribble
⟶ sprint
⊕ ball
⌂ cone

CONTRIBUTOR: Rick Dell, Men's Coach, Trenton State College, Trenton, New Jersey

Four vs. Two Shooting Intervals

FOCUS	AREA	PERSONNEL	EQUIPMENT
Shooting	44 × 36 yards	14 players	1 ball
Passing			2 goals
			6 vests

FORMATION: There are two teams of six players and a goalkeeper on each team. One team wears vests. Four defenders and the goalkeeper from one team and two attackers from the opposite team are in each part of a double penalty area. One team has a ball. The players are restricted to their own areas.

PROCEDURE: One team interpasses four vs. two. Defenders take shots on goal at any time from the farther penalty area with the two attackers on their team in the near penalty area looking for rebounds and deflections. The drill is done in 2-minute intervals or until a goal is scored with a 2-minute rest period if the play goes 2 minutes. Players change roles at each new interval.

VARIATIONS: 1. Players use unlimited touches.
2. Players use two touches.
3. Teams must make at least three passes before taking a shot.

A attacker
D defender
G goalkeeper
– – –▶ pass
-------▶ shot
⊗ ball

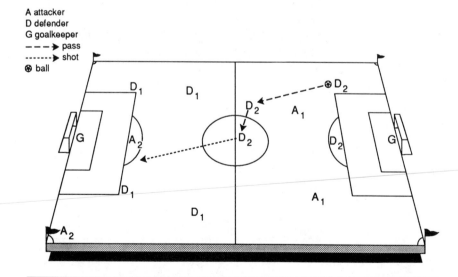

CONTRIBUTOR: Sigi Schmid, Men's Coach, University of California at Los Angeles, Los Angeles, California

Full-Pressure Midfield

FOCUS	AREA	PERSONNEL	EQUIPMENT
Attack	70 × 60 yards	18 players	1 ball
		1 coach	4 cones
			2 goals
			18 vests

FORMATION: Each team consists of three midfielders, three defenders, two strikers, and a goalkeeper. Teams wear different colored vests. The midfielders match up one vs. one in a 20-yard area marked by four cones set up 10 yards from midfield on each sideline. The strikers are matched against the opposing defenders in the appropriate areas between the cones and the 18-yard line. Portable goals are on each end line with a goalkeeper in each goal. The coach, with a ball, is outside the mid-field area.

PROCEDURE: The coach starts play by tossing the ball into the midfield area. The midfielders play three vs. three and can pass the ball forward to their strikers or back to their defenders or goalkeeper. All players must stay within their own areas. The ball must never bypass the midfield players. Goalkeepers can only throw the ball, and sidelines out-of-bounds play is restarted by throw-ins. Play continues until an attack is finished, after which the coach restarts play at midfield.

VARIATIONS: 1. Use a one- or two-touch restriction.
2. Require a back or midfielder to overlap any pass forward out of his or her area.
3. Require diagonal runs by strikers or midfielders before they receive through passes.
4. Make the field smaller.

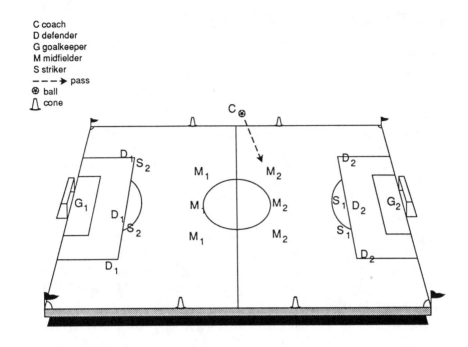

C coach
D defender
G goalkeeper
M midfielder
S striker
− − −▸ pass
⊕ ball
⌂ cone

CONTRIBUTOR: Suzanne Zaloom, Women's Coach, Union College, Schenectady, New York

Game for Possession

FOCUS	AREA	PERSONNEL	EQUIPMENT
Possession	30 to 40 × 50	14 players	7 balls
Shooting	to 60 yards		2 goals
Transition			7 vests

FORMATION: Twelve players are positioned within a 30 to 40 × 50 to 60 yard grid. A player on team D has the ball. Team D (with colored vests) has seven players, mainly backs and midfielders; team A (no vests) has five players, mainly strikers and an extra, or attacking, midfielder. A portable goal is on each end line with a goalkeeper in each goal. Extra balls are by each goal.

PROCEDURE: Team D gets 1 point for 10 consecutive passes. Their emphasis is on possession. Team A can try to score by shooting at either of the two goals. They get 1 point for each goal scored. When the ball goes out, team A gets it every time. Play continues for a designated time or number of goals.

VARIATIONS: 1. Team D can be assigned touch restriction—two touch, and so on.
2. Vary the number of players.
3. Vary the size of the area.

CONTRIBUTOR: Tom Griffith, Women's Coach, Princeton University, Princeton, New Jersey

Gauntlet

FOCUS	AREA	PERSONNEL	EQUIPMENT
Attack	Five 10 × 10	15-25 players	7 balls
Defense	yard grids		

FORMATION: Two vertical lines of attackers are on opposite sides at one end of a 10 × 10 yard grid. Each player in one line has a ball. A defender is in each of five grids in a row.

PROCEDURE: Two attackers enter the first grid and try to beat D1, who cannot leave the area. If successful, they move on to the next grid and take on D2, and so on. Every time they beat a defender they get a point. As attacking players progress they gain points. Defenders only have to knock the ball out of the grid area to stop the attack. Each time the defenders stop an attack, they move up a space, changing places with the defenders in the grids in front of them. The defenders become attackers by stopping an attack in the first grid. When this happens, the attackers who lost the ball go into the last grid and become defenders, and the successful defenders in the first grid go to the end of the attacking lines. A predetermined number of points wins.

VARIATIONS: 1. Use more grids—up to eight (80 yards).
2. Put limitations on the number of touches or make attacking players use wall passes only.

A attacker
D defender
⊕ ball

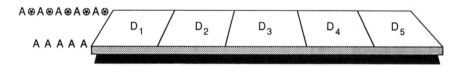

CONTRIBUTOR: Jack Writer, Assistant Athletic Director, Cornell University, Ithaca, New York

"Gechtman" Drill

FOCUS	AREA	PERSONNEL	EQUIPMENT
Receiving	20 × 20 yards	3 players	1 ball
Turning			2 cones
			2 flags
			1 goal

FORMATION: Two flags 3 feet apart are placed in the middle of a 20 × 20 yard grid. Two attackers, A1 and A2, are about 10 yards apart on opposite sides of the flags. A2 has a ball. On A2's side of the grid two cones are placed 3 feet from each flag. A goalkeeper is in a portable goal on the end of the grid behind A1.

PROCEDURE: A1 sprints to receive a pass from A2 between the flags. A1 dribbles toward A2 just past the cones and turns with the ball to face the goal. A2 makes an overlap run, receives a square pass from A1, dribbles, and finishes with a shot on goal. A1 and A2 rotate positions and continue the drill.

VARIATIONS:
1. Use one- and two-touch passes and shots.
2. A1 feints one way and passes to the opposite side.
3. Have a number of groups work at the same time.

A attacker
F feeder
G goalkeeper
⌇⟶ dribble
--→ pass
······→ shot
⟶ sprint
⊕ ball
⌂ cone
⚑ flag

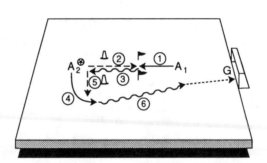

CONTRIBUTOR: Jay Gavitt, Girls' Coach, Columbia High School, Maplewood, New Jersey

Goalkeeper Catchall

FOCUS	AREA	PERSONNEL	EQUIPMENT
Goalkeeping	1/3 field	5 players	4 balls
Shooting		1 coach	1 goal
Passing			

FORMATION: A goalkeeper is in the goal. Another goalkeeper is behind the goal serving as a retriever. Three players and a coach, each with a ball, are outside the penalty area—X1 and X2 facing their near post, the coach in the middle, and X3 about 10 yards behind the coach.

PROCEDURE: In order, X1 shoots to the near post; X2 shoots to the near post; the coach delivers a ball to the top of the box, forcing the goalkeeper out of the goal; and X3 chips to the goal, forcing the goalkeeper back. The goalkeepers alternate after three to five repetitions.

VARIATION: Add two players, one on each side of the penalty area, to cross balls on goal.

C coach
G goalkeeper
X field player
------▶ shot
⊛ ball

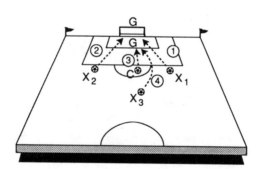

CONTRIBUTOR: Dr. Joseph A. Machnik, No. 1 Goalkeepers Camp, Guilford, Connecticut

Goalkeeper Distribution $\boxed{50}$

FOCUS	AREA	PERSONNEL	EQUIPMENT
Goalkeeping	1/2 field	6 players	6 balls
			8 cones
			1 goal

FORMATION: A goalkeeper is in the goal. A feeder with six balls is at the top of the penalty area. Four pairs of cones are set up in a semi-circle target area within the half-field area. A retriever stands outside each target.

PROCEDURE: The feeder serves a ball to the goalkeeper, who saves the ball and distributes it through one of the cone targets. The goalkeeper must use a different method to distribute each save.

VARIATIONS: 1. Use attackers and defenders instead of cones.
2. Vary the type and speed of each serve.
3. The goalkeeper saves shots on goal instead of serves.

F feeder
G goalkeeper
R retriever
‑ ‑ ‑ ▶ pass
⊕ ball
⌂ cone

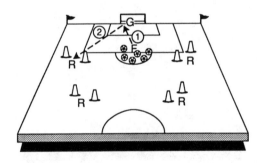

CONTRIBUTOR: Bill Vigor, Boys' Coach, Wheeler High School, Marietta, Georgia

GSC Passing Drill

FOCUS	AREA	PERSONNEL	EQUIPMENT
Passing	15 × 15 yards	6+ players	5 balls
Receiving		2 feeders	
Movement			
with/without			
the ball			

FORMATION: Two stationary feeders, F1 and F2, with two balls each are at the corners of a 15 × 15 yard grid. Two lines, A and B, with three players each are at the opposite corners facing each other. A player in line A has a ball.

PROCEDURE: The first player in line A passes to line B. After the pass, A cuts diagonally toward F1 and one touches a pass from F1 back to F1. Following this pass, A circles F1 and sprints to the end of line B. The B player controls the ball received from A and passes it back to the next player in line A. B then cuts toward F2 for a one-touch pass, circles F2, and goes to the end of line A. The drill continues for 5 minutes.

VARIATIONS: 1. Feeders can pick up the ball and have cutters head the ball back to them.
2. Feeders can serve the ball so cutters have to volley the ball back to them.

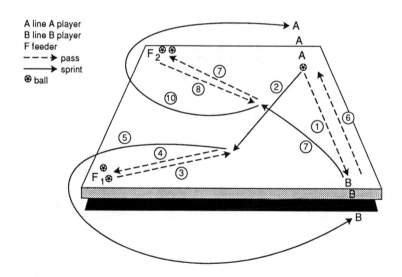

A line A player
B line B player
F feeder
– – –▶ pass
———▶ sprint
⊕ ball

CONTRIBUTOR: Daniel Gilmore, Men's Coach, Glassboro State College, Glassboro, New Jersey

53

HB Shooting

FOCUS	AREA	PERSONNEL	EQUIPMENT
Shooting	1/2 field	12 players	1 ball
Passing			2 cones
			1 goal
			5 vests

FORMATION: Five defenders wearing vests and one goalkeeper defend the regulation goal at one end of a half-field area. Six attackers, one with a ball, are at the other end. Two cones mark a goal at that end.

PROCEDURE: The six attackers try to work a player free for a shot on goal. All shots by the attackers will result in a goal, goalie save, or corner kick; no goal kicks. Defenders may score by passing the ball through the cones.

VARIATIONS: 1. Have two sets of goals for the defenders to score in.
2. Attackers use two-touch passing.

A attacker
D defender
G goalkeeper
⊕ ball
⩘ cone

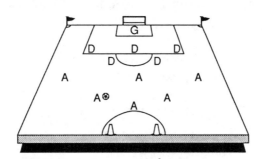

CONTRIBUTOR: Joseph Mancarella, Men's Coach, Monroe Community College, Rochester, New York

Head With Direction

FOCUS	AREA	PERSONNEL	EQUIPMENT
Heading	Any area	2 players	1 ball
Fitness			

FORMATION: One player holding a ball stands 5 yards from another player.

PROCEDURE: X1, with the ball, tosses the ball to X2, who heads it back to X1, who has started to run counterclockwise around X2. X1 then heads the ball back to X2, who turns to meet and return the ball. This continues for 1 minute in each direction. After 2 minutes players exchange roles.

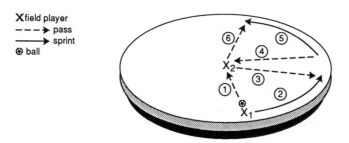

CONTRIBUTOR: Jerry Yeagley, Men's Coach, Indiana University, Bloomington, Indiana

High, Wide, and Far

FOCUS	AREA	PERSONNEL	EQUIPMENT
Heading	1/4 field	5+ players	8 balls
Fitness			1 goal

FORMATION: One player stands in the goal on the goal line. Four feeders, each with two balls, are located at various spots 6 to 12 yards outside the penalty area. Other players can serve as retrievers.

PROCEDURE: D runs to head eight balls served one at a time by the feeders. D tries to clear each ball outside the penalty box and returns to the goal line after heading each ball. The feeders alternate short and long passes. After eight passes the players rotate clockwise to new positions.

D defender
F feeder
R retriever
⊛ ball

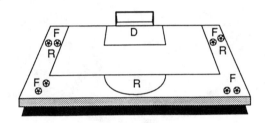

CONTRIBUTOR: John Boles, Men's Coach, Temple University, Philadelphia, Pennsylvania

Hitters and Dodgers

FOCUS	AREA	PERSONNEL	EQUIPMENT
Dribbling	Center circle	8+ players	8+ balls
Passing			
Fun			

FORMATION: All players are inside the center circle. Three players each have a ball. Enough balls for the remaining players are placed around the outside of the circle.

PROCEDURE: The players with the balls are hitters. They dribble inside the circle and attempt to pass at any player who doesn't have a ball while the players without balls try to avoid being hit. When hit below the waist, the hit player retrieves a ball from outside the circle and joins the hitters. The last three players hit are the winners and become the initial hitters in the next game.

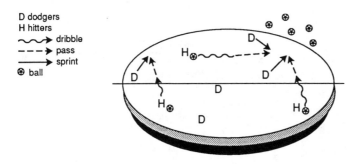

CONTRIBUTOR: Bob Warming, Men's Coach, Creighton University, Omaha, Nebraska

Hold That Ball

FOCUS	AREA	PERSONNEL	EQUIPMENT
Shielding	10 × 10 yards	4 players	1 ball
Support			4 cones
Defense			3 vests

FORMATION: Three attackers wearing vests and one defender are within a 10 × 10 yard grid bordered by four cones. One of the attackers has a ball.

PROCEDURE: Each attacker must keep possession of the ball by shielding and dribbling within the grid for at least 5 seconds before passing to another attacker. The defender attempts to win the ball, kick the ball out of bounds, or force the defender to dribble out of bounds. After a set time, one attacker switches with the defender.

VARIATIONS:
1. Add another defender and increase the size of the area to 15 × 15 yards.
2. The player holding the ball must convert a wall pass before passing to another player.
3. An attacker without the ball must use a takeover to gain possession of the ball.

A attacker
D defender
∿➔ dribble
--➔ pass
➔ sprint
⊕ ball
∆ cone

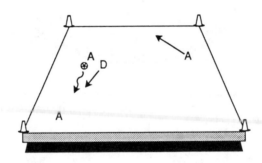

CONTRIBUTOR: Joseph Eck, Men's Coach, Sangamon State University, Springfield, Illinois

Keep-Away

FOCUS	AREA	PERSONNEL	EQUIPMENT
Passing	10 × 10 yards	5 players	1 ball
Receiving			4 cones

FORMATION: Four attackers, one with a ball, are outside a 10 × 10 yard grid marked by cones. One defender is in the middle.

PROCEDURE: The attackers interpass the ball while the defender attempts to intercept. The defender cannot come out of the grid. Attackers cannot enter the grid. Attacking players must play the ball first time (one touch).

VARIATIONS: 1. Add a fake before passing.
2. Add a second defender who must stay outside the cones.
3. Rotate players.

A attacker
D defender
– – –▸ pass
———▸ sprint
⊕ ball
⌂ cone

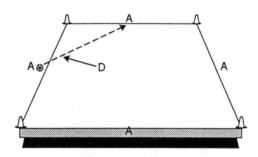

CONTRIBUTOR: Denise Dallamora, Women's Coach, Brandeis University, Waltham, Massachusetts

Keep-Away and Chip

FOCUS	AREA	PERSONNEL	EQUIPMENT
Passing	70 × 30 yards	13 players	6 balls
Movement with/without the ball		1 coach	6 vests

FORMATION: Team X and team Y have six players each. One team wears vests. Three players from each team are in each of two 30 × 30 yard grids. A goalkeeper stands in a 10-yard area between the grids. A coach with a supply of balls is located outside the middle area.

PROCEDURE: The coach passes to either grid. The two teams in that grid play three vs. three, trying to amass consecutive passes or making a chip pass to a teammate in the other grid, where the keep-away continues. Five consecutive passes equal 1 point. A chip to the other grid that is controlled by a teammate counts as 2 points. If the goalkeeper catches a chip, a point is deducted from the team whose player attempted the chip. As soon as a ball goes out of the grid, the coach passes another ball to either grid.

VARIATIONS: 1. Add players and increase the size of the area.
2. Play one, two, or three touch.
3. Have one goalkeeper for each team.

C coach
G goalkeeper
X, Y field players
⊕ ball

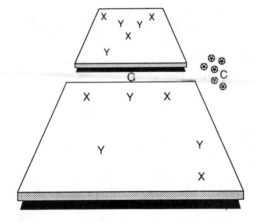

CONTRIBUTOR: Darryl Metcalfe, Boys' Coach, Westfield High School, Houston, Texas

Link Ten

FOCUS	AREA	PERSONNEL	EQUIPMENT
Attack	1/2 field	15 players	1 ball
Possession			1 goal
			8 vests

FORMATION: One group of eight defenders wearing vests, a goalkeeper, and a group of six attackers are spread out in a half-field area. The goalkeeper is in the goal with a ball.

PROCEDURE: The drill is basically nine vs. six play. The goalkeeper begins play with a goal kick within the half field. The defenders attempt to make 10 consecutive passes and cross midfield with a pass or dribble. The defenders count out each successful pass. The six attackers pressure the defenders to win the ball and, if successful, move to attack and shoot on goal. The defenders receive 1 point for successfully linking 10 passes and crossing midfield. The attackers receive 1 point for a shot on goal that is saved and 2 points for a goal. The first group to score 10 points wins, after which players rotate positions.

A attacker
D defender
G goalkeeper
– – –➤ pass
⊕ ball

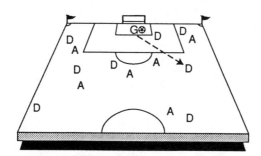

CONTRIBUTOR: Richard Burns, Women's Coach, Mount Holyoke College, South Hadley, Massachusetts

Luc's Drill

FOCUS	AREA	PERSONNEL	EQUIPMENT
Possession	20 × 20 yards	10 players	1 ball
Combination work			5 vests
Fitness			

FORMATION: There are two groups of five players. One group wears vests. Three players from team X and two players from team Y are within a 20 × 20 yard grid outlined by the remaining players. A team X player has a ball.

PROCEDURE: The teams play keep-away for 45-second sessions. Possession changes with a won ball or misplayed pass out of the grid. The group of three pass only among themselves. The group of two can pass between themselves and use any of their resting teammates as one-touch assistants. Active and resting players switch positions after each session.

VARIATIONS: 1. Decrease the size of the grid.
2. Play for longer periods.

X, Y field players
- - - ➤ pass
——➤ sprint
⊕ ball

CONTRIBUTOR: Robby Searl, Men's Coach, Nazareth College, Rochester, New York

Man Up, Man Down

FOCUS	AREA	PERSONNEL	EQUIPMENT
Passing	30 × 20 yards	5 players	1 ball
Dribbling			4 cones
			4 vests

FORMATION: Two teams of two players each face each other in the area. Teams wear different colored vests. One player has a ball. A free player, Z, is also in the area. Goals are marked by cones 4 feet apart.

PROCEDURE: This is a three vs. two game. The free player always plays with the team that has possession of the ball. The team scoring the most goals in a set time wins.

VARIATION: Play two vs. one, four vs. three, five vs. four, and so on. Vary the field size accordingly.

X, Y, Z field players
⊛ ball
⛆ cone

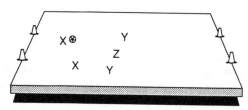

CONTRIBUTOR: Gary Parsons, Men's Coach, Oakland University, Rochester, Michigan

Movement Without the Ball

FOCUS	AREA	PERSONNEL	EQUIPMENT
Passing Movement with/without the ball	Three 20 × 20 yard grids	8 players	1 ball

FORMATION: Three 20 × 20 yard grids are within 5 yards of each other. One grid is empty; each of the other two grids is occupied by three attackers. An attacker in one grid has a ball. Two defenders are between the grids.

PROCEDURE: The three attackers with the ball play two-touch keep-away inside the grid until they are ready to serve to the next grid. The two defenders pressure all the grids but never enter a grid. Once the ball is served to another grid, the player who passed the ball follows the pass while the other two run into the empty grid. Now there are four players with a ball in one grid and two players in another grid. The four players with the ball now play keep-away. If they successfully make a pass to the other occupied grid, the player making the pass joins the two attackers receiving the ball. Three attackers now play keep-away. Play continues until a defender intercepts a pass. Thus all attackers are constantly moving with the ball.

VARIATIONS: 1. Use a one-touch restriction.
2. Balls must be served in the air into grids.

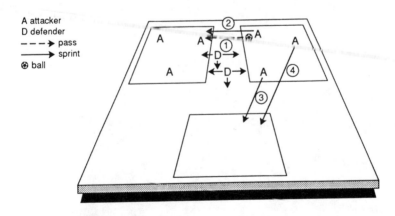

A attacker
D defender
– – –▸ pass
——▸ sprint
⊛ ball

CONTRIBUTOR: Bob Gray, Men's Coach, Alderson Broaddus College, Philippi, West Virginia

Nine vs. Nine Possession

FOCUS	AREA	PERSONNEL	EQUIPMENT
Attack	Full field	18 players	1 ball
Defense			2 goals
			8 vests

FORMATION: Two teams, each with three defenders, three midfielders, two attackers, and one goalkeeper, are in a full field. One team has the ball. One team wears vests.

PROCEDURE: The team with possession tries to score a goal. A team scores a goal by completing 10 consecutive passes or by scoring an actual soccer goal. The team that is behind must always try to score an actual goal. When the score is even, each team in sequence tries to score an actual goal until one team leads by two goals. The team with a two-goal lead may then score by completing 10 consecutive passes.

A attacker
D defender
G goalkeeper
M midfielder
– – –➤ pass
⊕ ball

CONTRIBUTOR: Vernon Mummert, Men's Coach, Drew University, Madison, New Jersey

No Man's Land

FOCUS	AREA	PERSONNEL	EQUIPMENT
Passing	Penalty area	8 players	1 ball
			4 cones

FORMATION: Four cones mark an 8-yard-wide "no man's land" in the center of the penalty area. Three attackers and one defender are within the penalty area on each side of the no man's land. An attacker in one area has a ball.

PROCEDURE: The attackers interpass within their area while the defender pressures the player with the ball. The ball is passed in the air across the no man's land at the first opportunity. No one may leave his or her area. The attackers try to make as many passes as possible or maintain ball control for as long as possible. The defender changes places with the attacker whose pass he or she intercepts, and the new group continues the game.

A attacker
D defender
⊕ ball
⌂ cone

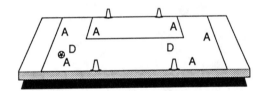

CONTRIBUTOR: Don A. Scarborough, Men's Coach, Brevard College, Brevard, North Carolina

Off and Out

FOCUS	AREA	PERSONNEL	EQUIPMENT
Goalkeeping	Penalty area	2 players	6 balls
Distribution		1 feeder	1 goal

FORMATION: One goalkeeper is on the end line in the goal. A feeder with a ball is about 20 yards out on one side of the field. A second goalkeeper is opposite the feeder on the other side of the field.

PROCEDURE: The feeder crosses a ball into the goal area so that the goalkeeper must come off the line (move to the ball) to collect the ball. Once in control of the ball the goalkeeper turns and distributes with an overarm pass to the other goalkeeper on the wing. The second goalkeeper collects the ball, then punts it across the field to the feeder. Continue the drill for a designated time after which the goalkeepers exchange positions.

VARIATION: Put one or more attackers in the middle to challenge the goalkeeper.

F feeder
G goalkeeper
– – –▶ pass
⊕ ball

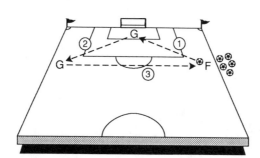

CONTRIBUTOR: Bret Owensby, Men's Coach, Concordia College, Portland, Oregon

Off the Ball Running

FOCUS	AREA	PERSONNEL	EQUIPMENT
Movement with/without the ball Passing	Full field	10 players	1 ball

FORMATION: Ten players, X1 to X10, are positioned in the middle of the field as indicated in the diagram. X3 has a ball.

PROCEDURE: The drill emphasizes moving without the ball and using the width of the field. To begin the drill X3 passes the ball to X5. Following a pass to X7, X5 moves to the right to receive the ball back from X7. As the key midfield player, X5's options are to play the ball to any of the forward players, who are making various runs. The object is to get the ball into the penalty area, after which the ball is brought back and players change positions.

VARIATIONS: 1. Add defenders.
2. Add a goalkeeper and finish the drill with a shot on goal.

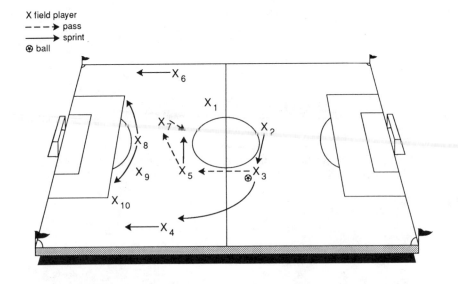

CONTRIBUTOR: Ron Crawford, Men's Coach, University of Southwestern Louisiana, Lafayette, Louisiana

Offense to Defense

FOCUS	AREA	PERSONNEL	EQUIPMENT
Attack	25 × 50 yards	10 to 14	4 balls
Defense		players	2 goals
Goalkeeping			

FORMATION: Two goals are positioned 25 yards apart. Four to six players line up behind the right post of each goal. A goalkeeper is in each goal. Two balls are at each right post.

PROCEDURE: Player X1 attacks and is defended by player X5. After either scoring or losing possession X1 becomes a defender. X5, after winning possession or receiving a ball distributed by the goalkeeper, becomes an attacker attacking the opposite goal. Each player completes one offensive and one defensive opportunity. Players go to the end of the opposite line on completion of their offensive and defensive turns.

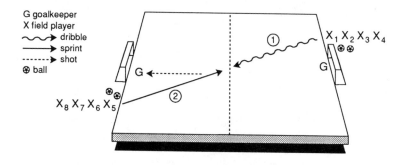

G goalkeeper
X field player
dribble
sprint
shot
ball

CONTRIBUTOR: Luis A. Sagastume, Men's Coach, United States Air Force Academy, Colorado Springs, Colorado

Offensive Heading

FOCUS	AREA	PERSONNEL	EQUIPMENT
Heading	10 × 10 yards	4 players	1 ball
Attack			2 vests
Fitness			

FORMATION: Two teams, each with two players, position themselves on opposite sides of a 10 × 10 yard grid. One team has possession of a ball. One team wears vests.

PROCEDURE: One player serves the ball to his or her teammate, who attempts to score by heading the ball past the opponents. The opponents save the ball and counterattack using the same serving procedure. Each goal scored counts as 1 point.

VARIATIONS: 1. The serve can be an underhand toss for less skilled players or a chip for more skilled players.

2. Require two or three head ball passes between teammates before a shot.

X, Y field players
– – –➤ pass
·······➤ shot (head)
⊕ ball

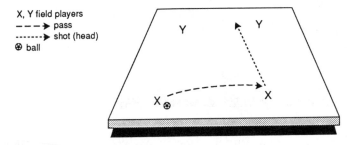

CONTRIBUTOR: Michelle Morgan, Women's Coach, Amherst College, Amherst, Massachusetts

One Blind Monkey

FOCUS	AREA	PERSONNEL	EQUIPMENT
Control	10 × 20 yards	4 players	1 ball
Deception			
Vision			

FORMATION: X1, with a ball, and X4 are on opposite end lines of a 10 × 20 yard grid. X2 and X3 are at the midline of the grid, X2 facing X1 and X3 facing X4.

PROCEDURE: X1 must beat X2 and X3 (whose back is turned) with a pass to X4. As soon as the ball passes X3, X3 pressures X4, who controls and tries to beat X3 and covering defender X2 (with back turned) with a pass back to X1. No balls may be played first time.

VARIATIONS: 1. Vary the length of the grid.
2. Do not allow a tackle until the ball has been touched.

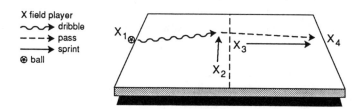

X field player
∿→ dribble
-- -→ pass
——→ sprint
⊕ ball

CONTRIBUTOR: Curtis Lauber, Men's Coach, Swarthmore College, Swarthmore, Pennsylvania

One Touch

FOCUS	AREA	PERSONNEL	EQUIPMENT
Attack	Penalty area	11 players	1 ball
Passing			1 goal
			10 vests

FORMATION: Two teams of five players each plus one midfielder, who plays for the team in possession of the ball, are within the penalty area. A player on one team has a ball. The two teams wear different colored vests.

PROCEDURE: Play five vs. five plus one midfielder for the team with the ball. Unlimited touches are permitted; however, 1 point is scored for every one-touch pass. Twenty points wins a game. Points can be scored only by completing one-touch passes between teammates.

VARIATIONS: 1. Play five vs. five plus one. All players play two-touch except the midfielder, who must play one-touch.
2. Play four vs. four plus one.
3. Play three vs. three plus one. A one-touch pass, a one-two pass, or a takeover equals 1 point.

X, Y field players
M midfielder
⊕ ball

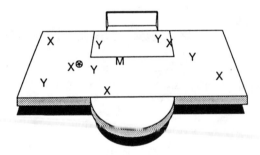

CONTRIBUTOR: Bob Dikranian, Assistant Men's Coach, Southern Connecticut State University, New Haven, Connecticut

One-Touch Shooting

FOCUS	AREA	PERSONNEL	EQUIPMENT
Shooting	Penalty area	3 players	10 balls
Fitness			1 cone
Goalkeeping			1 goal
Passing			

FORMATION: A goalkeeper is in the goal and an attacker is in the goal area near the far post. A cone is on the 6-yard line corner opposite the shooter. A feeder with 10 balls is at the corner of the 18-yard line opposite the shooter.

PROCEDURE: The attacker receives 10 consecutive passes at a rapid pace. The shooter attempts a one-touch shot of each pass and must sprint around the cone after each shot. The feeder should vary the passes. The goalkeeper should try not to overplay the attacker but play as if the feeder is a potential shooter, then adjust to block the attacker after the feeder passes the ball.

VARIATIONS: 1. Put a defender on the shooter.
2. Have the feeder receive each ball from a coach for quick control and pass.

A attacker
F feeder
G goalkeeper
– – –▶ pass
······▶ shot
———▶ sprint
⊛ ball
⋀ cone

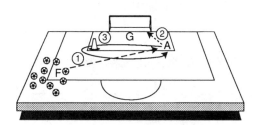

CONTRIBUTOR: Harry Fleishman, Boys' Coach, Shady Side Academy, Pittsburgh, Pennsylvania

One vs. One—Attack

FOCUS	AREA	PERSONNEL	EQUIPMENT
Attack	Penalty area	14 players	4 balls
Defense			1 goal

FORMATION: Four vertical lines of three attackers each are spread across the penalty area facing the goal. The first player in each line has a ball. A defender is positioned in the penalty area. A goalkeeper is in the goal.

PROCEDURE: Play begins with the first player in line A1 moving to attack D. They play one vs. one, A1 trying to score and the defender trying to win the ball. Play continues until A1 scores or the ball leaves the 18-yard area. The goalkeeper assists the defender with shouted directions. The instant that A1 scores or the ball leaves the box, A2 attacks the same defender, who must recover and play defense; in the same manner A3 and finally A4 all quickly attack the same defender. Once four players have attacked, the defender changes places with any attacker who has not yet been a defender and play continues.

A attacker
D defender
G goalkeeper
~~➤ dribble
──➤ sprint
⊕ ball

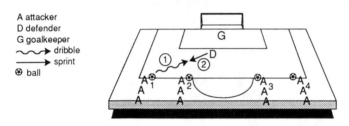

CONTRIBUTOR: Michael Coven, Men's Coach, Brandeis University, Waltham, Massachusetts

One vs. One—Defense

FOCUS	**AREA**	**PERSONNEL**	**EQUIPMENT**
Defense	10 × 20 yards	2 players	1 ball

FORMATION: One attacker (A) and one defender (D) with a ball are positioned at each end of a 10 × 20 yard grid.

PROCEDURE: D makes a good firm pass to A, who must wait for the pass on the end line. D quickly follows the pass, trying to close the attacker's space. D should channel A, trying to deny forward movement. D should be patient and learn to find the appropriate time to strip A of the ball. (*Do not* lunge for the ball.) Play stops when D gets the ball or A dribbles over D's end line.

VARIATIONS:
1. Place a time restriction on the attacker trying to get to the other end line.
2. Force the attacker to use his or her nondominant foot.
3. The defender should not tackle but should try to deny forward progress by getting in front of the attacker's dribble and shielding and winning the ball.

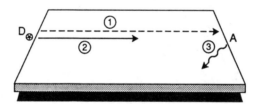

CONTRIBUTOR: Randall May, Women's Coach, Cornell University, Ithaca, New York

One vs. One— Four Corner Players

FOCUS	AREA	PERSONNEL	EQUIPMENT
Shielding	20 × 20 yards	6 players	1 ball
Passing			

FORMATION: A 20 × 20 yard grid is determined by four players, each on the corner of the square. Two other players, one with a ball, are inside the square.

PROCEDURE: The player with the ball retains possession by interpassing with the four players positioned at the corners. The opponent in the middle tries to win the ball. The middle players change with two corner players after a designated period.

VARIATIONS: 1. Use a one-touch restriction.
2. The corner players can play to each other if the middle player is marked.

A attacker
D defender
X field player
– – –▶ pass
———▶ sprint
⊛ ball

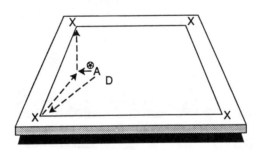

CONTRIBUTOR: Mike Rubesch, Men's Coach, Emory University, Atlanta, Georgia

One vs. One Plus

FOCUS	AREA	PERSONNEL	EQUIPMENT
Attack	10 × 20 yards	6 players	6 balls
Defense			3 vests

FORMATION: Two groups of three players each are positioned in a 10 × 20 yard grid. One player from each team is in the middle, one support player is on each sideline, and one "target/goal" player is on each end line. One group wears vests. One player in the middle has a ball.

PROCEDURE: X1 and Y1 play one vs. one. The objective is to score into the opponent's goal (i.e., between the legs of X2 or Y2, who stand facing playing area with legs about 3 feet apart). X3 and Y3 can move only back and forth along their respective sidelines and are restricted to one touch. However, they may play with whoever has possession of the ball. X3 and Y3 "show" for a wall pass. Play continues for a set period, after which players are rotated numerically.

VARIATION: Play with full-size goals and goalkeepers instead of the end players.

X, Y field players
〜〜➤ dribble
———➤ sprint
⊕ ball

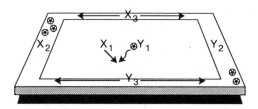

CONTRIBUTOR: T. Barry Gorman, Men's Coach, Pennsylvania State University, University Park, Pennsylvania

77

Overhead Bicycle Kick

FOCUS	AREA	PERSONNEL	EQUIPMENT
Shooting	25 yards	2 players	Balls
			2 cones
			Padded mats

FORMATION: The attacker stands in front of a padded mat placed in front of a target (two cones). A ball thrower or feeder is 5 to 10 yards in front of the attacker.

PROCEDURE: The feeder or thrower tosses or kicks a ball over the head of the attacker. In jumping, the attacker's kicking leg is swung above the head, meeting the ball above the head. By placing the palms down, the kicker uses the hands to help break the fall before he or she lands on the mat. Caution: Be certain to use protective mats, and use this drill only with advanced players.

VARIATIONS:
1. Remove the mat after the player learns the technique of falling.
2. After removing the mat use a defender and/or goalkeeper behind the kicker.
3. The feeder should kick the ball from different angles.
4. Create game situations.

A attacker
F feeder
– – –➤ pass
------➤ shot
⊕ ball
⌂ cone

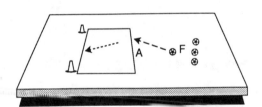

CONTRIBUTOR: Ata Razani & Biren Hodges, Boys' Coaches, Northglenn High School, Northglenn, Colorado

Overlap

FOCUS	AREA	PERSONNEL	EQUIPMENT
Overlapping Attack Passing	Full field	5 players	2 balls 2 goals

FORMATION: A goalkeeper is in each goal, a defender is in front of the goal, an attacker is upfield by the touchline, and a midfielder is upfield closer to the center of the field. The goalkeeper has a ball.

PROCEDURE: The defender runs to receive the ball distributed by the goalkeeper. The defender passes up to the attacker, who passes to the midfielder. The defender overlaps upfield along the touchline. The midfielder passes upfield to the defender. The midfielder and the attacker go inside and forward for a cross from the defender. The ball is passed over the touch line or a shot is taken. This same group goes down the field the opposite way following a goalkeeper pass.

VARIATIONS: 1. One touch and imaginative passes can be introduced to create different movements.

2. The first pass goes to the midfielder, who lays it back to the defender, and runs continue.

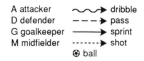

A attacker   ~~→ dribble
D defender   – – → pass
G goalkeeper   ——→ sprint
M midfielder   ······→ shot
        ⊛ ball

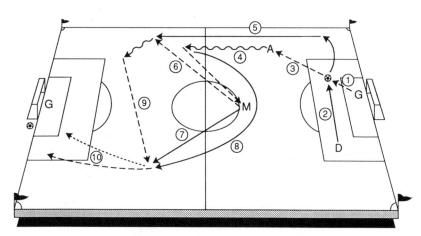

CONTRIBUTOR: Larry M. Gross, Women's Coach, North Carolina State University, Raleigh, North Carolina

Pass and Change

FOCUS	AREA	PERSONNEL	EQUIPMENT
Passing	15 × 15 yard	5 players	1 ball
Movement	grid		4 cones
with/without			
the ball			

FORMATION: One player, X5 is in the center of the grid, with a player in each of the area's corners. Any one of the corner players has a ball.

PROCEDURE: The drill can start in any corner—for example, X4 starts by passing to X5. X5 then passes to X1, after which X4 and X5 exchange positions. The drill continues in the same fashion around the area.

VARIATION: Use the following passing restrictions:

1. Two touch.
2. One touch.
3. Inside of foot.
4. Outside of foot.

X field player
- - - ➤ pass
———➤ sprint
⊕ ball
⌂ cone

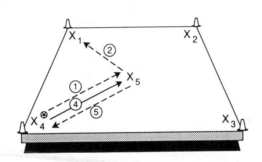

CONTRIBUTOR: Helmut Werner, Men's Coach, Randolph-Macon College, Ashland, Virginia

Pass and Receive Game

FOCUS	AREA	PERSONNEL	EQUIPMENT
Passing	30 × 40 yards	15 players	5 balls
Fitness			15 numbered vests

FORMATION: All players, wearing vests numbered 1 to 15, are positioned in a 30 × 40 yard area. Players numbered 1, 4, 7, 10, and 13 each have a ball.

PROCEDURE: All players begin jogging within the field area. Players with balls locate and pass to the player one number above them. The player with the highest number passes to number 1 to complete the cycle. After passing the ball, the players must be ready to receive a pass from the player one number below them. All players, with or without a ball, move continuously throughout the exercise. Play for 5 to 10 minutes.

VARIATIONS: 1. Add additional soccer balls.
2. Expand the space for longer passes.

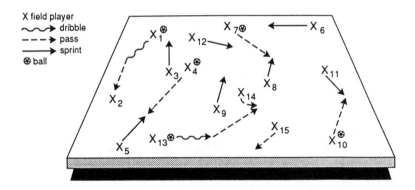

CONTRIBUTOR: Dr. Joe Luxbacher, Men's Coach, University of Pittsburgh, Pittsburgh, Pennsylvania

Pass-Collect-Shoot

FOCUS	AREA	PERSONNEL	EQUIPMENT
Warm-up	Full field	12 players	2 balls
Passing		4 feeders	2 goals
Shooting			
Dribbling			

FORMATION: Five players are in each of two lines at opposite corners of a full field. The first player in each line has a ball. There are two feeders on each side of the field, each one located 10 yards on either side of midfield. A goalkeeper is in each goal.

PROCEDURE: The first player in each line dribbles toward midfield and passes to the feeder on that side of midfield. The feeders make one-touch return passes to the players, who have continued toward midfield. The players repeat the same maneuver with the feeders on the other side of midfield; then the players dribble to the 18-yard line, shoot on goal, and run to the end of the opposite line. The balls are returned to the next players in line, who continue the drill.

VARIATIONS: 1. Place a striker in each penalty area and have the field players cross to them.
2. Place a defender on each striker.

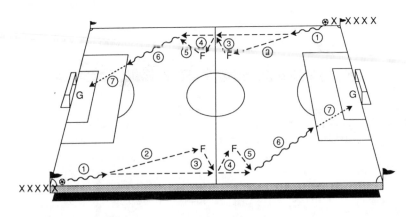

CONTRIBUTOR: Thomas Taylor, Boys' Coach, West Essex High School, North Caldwell, New Jersey

Passing for Points

FOCUS	AREA	PERSONNEL	EQUIPMENT
Passing	25 × 25 yards	6 to 12 players	3 to 6 balls
Shielding	to 35 × 35		
Communi-	yards		
cation			

FORMATION: Six to 12 players in pairs are within a 25 × 25 to 35 × 35 yard grid. Each pair has a ball.

PROCEDURE: The player in each pair without the ball initiates a diagonal run to receive a lead ground pass from the player with the ball. Players communicate visually, not verbally. The diagonal run begins when eye contact is made between the partners. Play continues for 45 seconds. A point is scored when a player receives and controls the ball on the run. A point is lost when the ball leaves the grid, does not reach the target, or hits another ball or player; or when the receiving player was not moving.

VARIATIONS: 1. Add one or two defenders. If the pass is intercepted, a point is lost; points are scored by the same method.
2. Add a goalkeeper as a defender (points are scored or lost as in the previous variation).

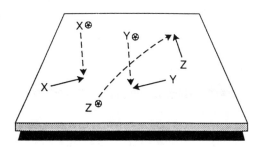

CONTRIBUTOR: TJ Kostecky, Men's Coach, New Jersey Tech, Newark, New Jersey

Passing in Order

FOCUS	AREA	PERSONNEL	EQUIPMENT
Support	20 × 20 yards	4 players	1 ball
Passing			
Receiving			

FORMATION: Four players, each assigned a number, are positioned randomly in the grid. One player (X1) has a ball.

PROCEDURE: All players are moving continuously in the grid. X1, with a ball, must pass to X2 (thus X2 concentrates on his or her support position while X3 and X4 take imaginary defenders away). X2 must then pass to X3, and so on.

VARIATIONS: 1. The next player takes the ball away instead of receiving a pass.
2. Do the same activity with no assigned numbers. Passes can be made randomly.
3. Use two balls.

X field player
~~~> dribble
---> pass
——> sprint
⊕ ball

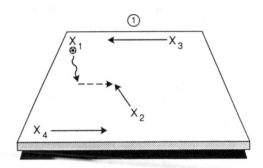

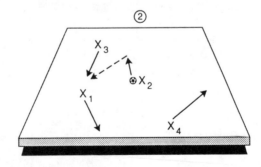

CONTRIBUTOR: John Werner, Boys' Coach, Arlington Memorial High School, Arlington, Vermont

Player Under Pressure

FOCUS	AREA	PERSONNEL	EQUIPMENT
Passing	10 × 10 yards	4 players	2 balls
Fitness			
Control			

FORMATION: One player is at each corner of a 10 × 10 yard grid. X1 is designated as the player under pressure. X3 and X4 each have a ball.

PROCEDURE: X4 passes to X1, who must pass to the player without a ball (X2). X3 immediately passes to X1, who again passes to the player without a ball (X4).The drill continues for 30 seconds, after which a different player is put under pressure. The coach keeps track of the number of balls played and the number of successful and unsuccessful passes.

VARIATIONS: 1. Use one- and two-touch restrictions.
2. Vary the types of passes.

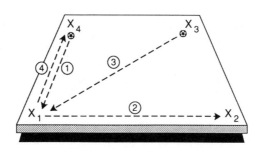

X field player
– – –▶ pass
⊕ ball

CONTRIBUTOR: Francis X. Reidy, Men's Coach, Saint Leo College, Saint Leo, Florida

Points Game

FOCUS	AREA	PERSONNEL	EQUIPMENT
Shooting	Penalty area	9 players	4 balls
Crossing		4 feeders	2 cones
Goalkeeping			1 goal
Clearing			

FORMATION: Two teams, X and Y, of six players each are positioned around the perimeter of the penalty area as shown in the diagram. The target zone is between the penalty mark and the goal area. Each team consists of two feeders, each with a ball, and four attackers. A cone is placed on each side of the penalty area a few yards inside the end line. A goalkeeper is in the goal.

PROCEDURE: A feeder from team X dribbles outside and past the cone, turns, and crosses a ball in the air to a target area between the penalty mark and the goal area. Two X players run in tandem toward the penalty area, timing their runs to meet the ball in the air for a head or volley shot on goal. Each player has a one-touch restriction. The feeders and attackers on each team and the teams alternate crosses and shots until each team has served 10 balls, after which the teams alternate sides of the field. Feeders must use the left foot from the left side and the right foot from the right side. The coach keeps score, awarding points as follows: diving header, 5; header, 4; full volley, 3; half volley, 2; rebound/deflection, 1.

VARIATIONS: 1. Add defenders.
2. Give points to the goalkeeper and defenders for winning balls.

G goalkeeper
F feeder
X, Y field players
〜〜➤ dribble
---➤ pass
——➤ sprint
······➤ shot
⊕ ball
⌂ cone

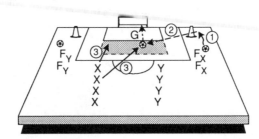

CONTRIBUTOR: Susan Ryan, Women's Coach, SUNY at Stony Brook, Stony Brook, New York

Possession Game

FOCUS	AREA	PERSONNEL	EQUIPMENT
Possession	40 × 40 yards	16 players	1 ball
Passing			8 vests
Support			

FORMATION: There are two teams of eight players each. One team wears vests. Four players from each team are inside a 40-yard grid, and four players on each team are around the perimeter of the grid. One player in the middle has a ball.

PROCEDURE: Play four vs. four inside the grid. The team in possession of the ball can utilize their wide teammates; however, the wide players are allowed only one touch, cannot play the ball back to the same player, cannot tackle, and cannot pass to another wide player. Ten consecutive passes equal one goal. Inside and wide players are rotated after each goal.

VARIATION: Restrict touches for inside players as desired.

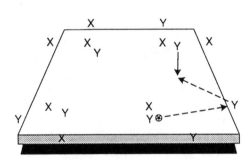

CONTRIBUTOR: Steve Allison, Men's Coach, Alfred University, Alfred, New York

Pressure Cooker

FOCUS	AREA	PERSONNEL	EQUIPMENT
Goalkeeping	Center circle or	11 players	1 ball
Passing	similar size		
Shooting	area		

FORMATION: Ten players position themselves around the center circle. A goalkeeper is inside the circle. One attacker has a ball.

PROCEDURE: Players on the circle keep the ball moving with one-touch passes. At any time a player can shoot at the goalkeeper. The goalkeeper must constantly anticipate a shot. After fielding a shot the goalkeeper returns the ball to one of the players on the circle.

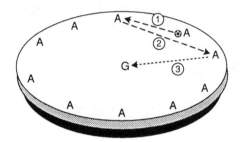

A attacker
G goalkeeper
– – –▶ pass
······▶ shot
⊕ ball

CONTRIBUTOR: Owen L. Wright, Men's Coach, University of La Verne, La Verne, California

Pressure Shooting

FOCUS	AREA	PERSONNEL	EQUIPMENT
Attack	30 × 30 yards	14 players	12 balls
Defense			2 goals
Fitness			12 vests

FORMATION: Two regulation goals are placed facing each other in a 30 × 30 yard area. Players are divided into teams of three, each team wearing different colored vests. Two teams are within the playing area. Teams not playing stand behind the goals and retrieve balls. A goalkeeper is in each goal. Six balls are placed in each net.

PROCEDURE: A goalkeeper distributes one ball into play and teams play three vs. three for 3 minutes, after which teams are rotated. The coach stipulates the touch limit; two- or three-touch works best. Goalkeepers are instructed to get balls in play as quickly as possible after each shot on goal.

VARIATIONS:
1. For problems scoring off crosses and outside services, make the width 70 yards, mark off a central 35-yard zone with cones, and play three-touch outside the cones and one-touch inside the cones.
2. For players overpassing in the box, allow unlimited touches but require a pass to a teammate before a shot.

G goalkeeper
W, X, Y, Z field players
– – – ► pass
⊕ ball

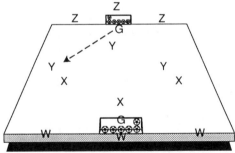

CONTRIBUTOR: Bill Coulthart, Men's Coach, Jacksonville University, Jacksonville, Florida

Pressure Turning

FOCUS	AREA	PERSONNEL	EQUIPMENT
Receiving	10 × 10 yards	4 players	1 ball

FORMATION: X2 stands between X1 and X3. X4 stands beside X2 providing passive pressure. X1 has a ball.

PROCEDURE: X1 passes to X2. The pass can be on the ground, or in the air to the thigh, chest, or head. On receiving the ball, X2 turns in one smooth movement and passes to X3. While X2 is doing this, X4 can pressure, and even bump, X2. After the pass to X3, X2 is facing X3 and awaits a return pass. On receiving the return pass, X2 turns and passes to X1. The drill continues in this fashion for a prescribed period, usually 1 minute, after which players change positions.

VARIATION: On the initial pass X1 can call for a return pass. X2 in this situation attempts to receive the ball, turn around, and return the ball to X1.

X field player
– – –▶ pass
———▶ sprint
⊕ ball

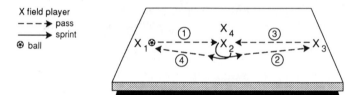

CONTRIBUTOR: Russ Fager, Men's Coach, Rider College, Trenton, New Jersey

Rapid-Fire Shooting

FOCUS	AREA	PERSONNEL	EQUIPMENT
Shooting	Full field	22 players	12 balls
Dribbling		2 feeders	2 goals
Goalkeeping			

FORMATION: Five players are lined up behind each corner flag of a 50-yard field. Two goals are on each end line with a goalkeeper in each goal. One feeder with six balls is on each sideline at midfield.

PROCEDURE: F1 makes alternate passes to lines 1 and 4. F2 alternately passes to lines 2 and 3. The players alternately sprint out of each line for shots on goal. The shooting players rotate lines (1 to 4, 4 to 1, 2 to 3, 3 to 2).

VARIATIONS:
1. Players use one touch shots.
2. Players play touch-control-shot.
3. Players use volley shots.
4. Player 4 passes to player 2, who shoots.
   Player 2 passes to player 4, who shoots.
   Player 1 passes to player 3, who shoots.
   Player 3 passes to player 1, who shoots.
5. The coach calls line numbers. The first player to the ball is the attacker and the second is the defender for one vs. one play.

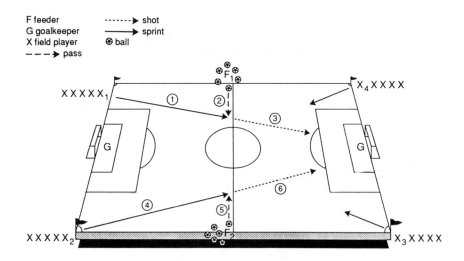

F feeder · · · · · · ▶ shot
G goalkeeper ──────▶ sprint
X field player ⊛ ball
– – – ▶ pass

CONTRIBUTOR: Gus Constantine, Men's Coach, New York University, New York, New York

Rhythm

FOCUS	AREA	PERSONNEL	EQUIPMENT
Passing	1/2 field	12 players	1 ball
Support			1 goal
			12 vests

FORMATION: Three teams of four players each are within the half-field area. Each team wears different colored vests. One of the teams has a ball.

PROCEDURE: One team is designated as defenders for eight vs. four keep-away. The objective is to maintain possession with short passes combined with cross-field passes. The team that turns the ball over, kicks it out of bounds, or puts a teammate in trouble with a bad pass becomes the defense.

VARIATIONS:
1. Restrict the number of touches—ideally to one touch.
2. The ball must be played with the inside or the outside of the foot only.
3. Combine variations 1 and 2.

X, Y, Z field players
– – – ▶ pass
———▶ sprint
⊕ ball

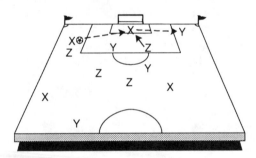

CONTRIBUTOR: Tom Turner, Men's Coach, Cleveland State University, Cleveland, Ohio

Rotation Shooting

FOCUS	AREA	PERSONNEL	EQUIPMENT
Shooting	Penalty area	7 players	10 balls
Fitness		1 feeder	1 goal
Goalkeeping			

FORMATION: Three players, X1, X2, and X3, position themselves in a triangle outside the penalty area arc. A feeder with a supply of balls stands near X2. A goalkeeper is in the goal. Three other players serve as retrievers behind the goal.

PROCEDURE: The feeder spots the ball for X2. X2 passes to X1 and sprints around the arc to take X1's position. X1 lays off a square pass for an oncoming X3 and moves to X3's position. X3 shoots first time on goal and moves to X2's position, where the feeder has placed another ball. The drill continues at full speed for 2 minutes, players attempting as many shots as possible. After 2 minutes, retrievers and shooters change positions.

VARIATION: Set up competition with 5 points for a goal and 1 point for a shot on goal that is saved.

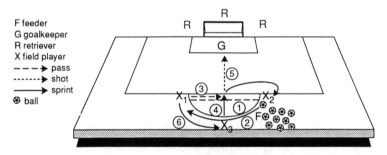

F feeder
G goalkeeper
R retriever
X field player
- - - ➤ pass
------- ➤ shot
——— ➤ sprint
⊕ ball

CONTRIBUTOR: Ed Nirrengarten, Boys' Coach, Avon High School, Indianapolis, Indiana

Run and Shoot

FOCUS	AREA	PERSONNEL	EQUIPMENT
Shooting	1/2 field	9 players	8 balls
Fitness			1 cone
			1 goal

FORMATION: Five players form a vertical line (X1) behind a cone about 40 yards from the goal. Two players, X2 and X3, each with a ball, are located opposite each other near each sideline about 30 yards from the goal. Another player, X4, with a ball is on the end line by a goalpost. Five balls are placed along the 18-yard line. A goalkeeper is in the goal.

PROCEDURE: The first X1 player sprints to X2 to receive an air pass. After returning the pass to X2, X1 sprints back to the cone and then on to X3. After receiving a ground pass from X3, X1 returns the pass and sprints forward to the 18-yard line, shoots one of the balls on goal, receives a pass from X4, returns the pass, and sprints back to the cone. The drill is repeated by each X1 player until all five balls are shot.

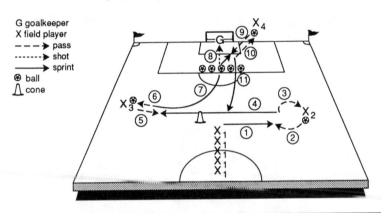

CONTRIBUTOR: Ronald R. Rudland, Boys' Coach, Western High School Parma, Michigan

Scramble

FOCUS	AREA	PERSONNEL	EQUIPMENT
Attack	1/2 field	21 players	8 balls
Reaction		1 coach	1 goal
			8 vests

FORMATION: A goalkeeper is in the net and four attackers are inside the penalty area along with three defenders. Four wings are outside the penalty area, two on each side of the field. Each wing has a ball. Four attackers are in a semicircle outside the penalty area. Other defenders stand behind the end line to serve as ball retrievers and defensive substitutes. The defenders wear vests. The coach has a supply of balls behind the end line.

PROCEDURE: A1 starts the drill by dribbling toward the end line. As this is done, the four attackers in the penalty area start to make runs inside the area, and the defenders move to cover. A1 crosses the ball inside the 18-yard line. The four attackers attempt to score while the defenders attempt to clear the ball. The four attackers outside the area send any loose balls back at the goal while the attackers inside the area look for rebounds. The coach can send a ball out to the players outside the area once the original ball has been cleared. A2, on the other side of the field, starts the next attack once play has stopped.

VARIATIONS: 1. Add more attackers and defenders.
2. Put a time limit on actual play (e.g., 20 seconds to score).
3. Instead of crossing from the end line, the coach sends balls in from steeper angles.
4. Attackers must make two passes before they can shoot.

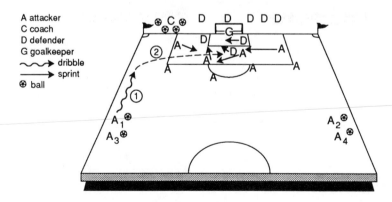

A attacker
C coach
D defender
G goalkeeper
〜〜➤ dribble
———➤ sprint
⊕ ball

CONTRIBUTOR: Ted Garber, Men's Coach, University of New Hampshire, Durham, New Hampshire

"Scramble" Drill

FOCUS	AREA	PERSONNEL	EQUIPMENT
Control	Penalty area	20 players	20 balls
Vision			

FORMATION: Twenty players, each with a ball, are within the penalty area.

PROCEDURE: The players begin dribbling within the area. On the coach's whistle, each player passes the ball to another player, receives another ball, and continues dribbling until the next whistle. Players should be aware of verbal and nonverbal cues so that only one person passes to each player per turn.

VARIATIONS:
1. Increase or decrease the size of the area and the number of players.
2. Use half the number of balls as players (e.g., for 10 players use five balls). The dribblers must now find a free player to pass to before receiving a pass.

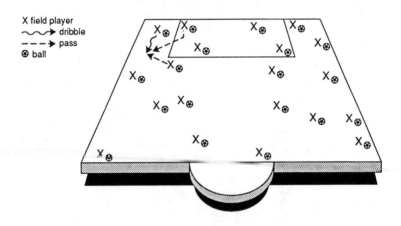

CONTRIBUTOR: Joe Bean, Men's Coach, Wheaton College, Wheaton, Illinois

Set Up

FOCUS	AREA	PERSONNEL	EQUIPMENT
Attack	1/2 field	3 players in	1 ball for each
Passing		each group	group
Control			
Shooting			

FORMATION: Two midfielders are about 30 yards apart near midfield. The left midfielder has a ball. An attacker is in the arc at the top of the penalty area. The remaining players are split into the three groups: the attackers standing behind the goal and the midfielders behind their respective positions.

PROCEDURE: The left midfielder (LM) dribbles across the field and passes to the right midfielder (RM), who is making a diagonal run. The RM controls the ball and dribbles toward the goal while the LM overlaps the RM on the right side. The RM passes to the LM, who one-touch passes to the attacker. The RM and LM overlap the attacker on the right and left, respectively. The attacker passes to either player, who takes a shot on goal. Following each shot, the players move to the end of their respective groups, and three new players repeat the drill.

VARIATIONS: 1. The midfielders make straight runs instead of cross-ing runs.
2. Add defenders.

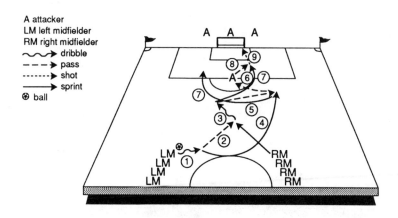

A attacker
LM left midfielder
RM right midfielder
~~~> dribble
---> pass
------> shot
——> sprint
⊕ ball

CONTRIBUTOR: Fred Genge, Boys' Coach, Peoria High School, Peoria, Illinois

Shooting off a Target Player

FOCUS	AREA	PERSONNEL	EQUIPMENT
Passing	40 × 50 yards	10 players	1 ball
Penetration			4 cones
Shooting			2 goals

FORMATION: Divide the playing area in two with cones. A regulation goal is on each end line, about 50 yards apart. A goalkeeper is in each goal. Three defenders and one striker are in one half of the area, with three attackers and one defender in the other half. One of the three attackers has a ball.

PROCEDURE: The object is to play three vs. one and pass the ball to the striker (who is in a one vs. three situation), who must win the ball and lay it back to any of the attackers for a shot on goal. All players must stay in their half of the area. The ball must be played off the striker.

VARIATIONS: 1. Create a more realistic situation by adding players, making the field larger, and taking away the cones.
2. Eliminate the rule of playing off the striker; allow the striker to turn and shoot. Build play into a gamelike situation.

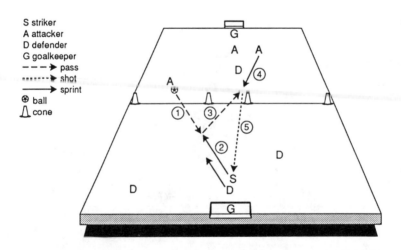

S striker
A attacker
D defender
G goalkeeper
– – –▶ pass
▪▪▪▪▪▶ shot
———▶ sprint
⊕ ball
⚠ cone

CONTRIBUTOR: I.M. Ibrahim, Men's Varsity Coach, and Greg Hooks, Assistant Coach, Clemson University, Clemson, South Carolina

Shooting on Goal

FOCUS	AREA	PERSONNEL	EQUIPMENT
Shooting	1/3 field	13 players	8 balls
Goalkeeping			4 cones
Fitness			1 goal

FORMATION: Six attackers form a vertical line behind a cone 15 yards beyond the center of the penalty area. Another cone is 10 yards nearer the penalty area. Another cone is on each side of the 18-yard line, with four balls spread outside each of those cones. A goalkeeper is in the goal. Six players serve as retrievers behind the goal.

PROCEDURE: Each player in turn sprints to the second cone, circles it, and moves to the right cone to shoot the four balls, using the right foot. After each shot, the player sprints around the cone before taking the next shot. After taking all four shots on the right, the player moves to the left cone and shoots each ball in the same manner, using the left foot. After all eight shots have been taken, the shooter switches with a retriever, who moves to the end of the attacking line. While the switch is taking place a retriever sprints to the eighteen yard line and sets the balls up for the next attacker. Other retrievers send balls to the eighteen yard line to be set up.

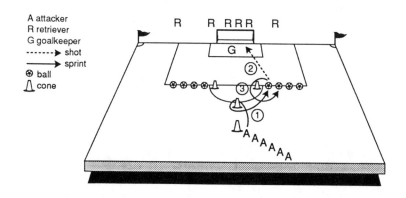

A attacker
R retriever
G goalkeeper
------▶ shot
——▶ sprint
⊗ ball
⚠ cone

CONTRIBUTOR: James R. Birmingham, Boys' Coach, Meadowbrook High School, Richmond, Virginia

Short Goal With Wall

FOCUS	AREA	PERSONNEL	EQUIPMENT
Wing play	1/2 field	12 players	1 ball
Defense			5 cones
Goalkeeping			2 goals

FORMATION: Two goals are 20 yards apart in the middle of a half field. Five cones form a 40-yard-wide wall midway between the goals. Five players are on each side of the wall. A goalkeeper is in each goal. One goalkeeper has a ball.

PROCEDURE: The goalkeeper puts the ball in play, and each team tries to score on the opposing goal. Players can travel through the wall but the ball must go around it. All of the half-field area is in bounds, so play can occur behind each goal. Goalkeepers can distribute the ball only by throwing it. Play is stopped only when (a) a goal is scored (the goalkeeper who was scored on restarts play with a pass to a teammate), (b) a foul is committed (play is restarted by an indirect kick at the point of the infraction, or (c) the ball crosses over or through the imaginary wall (play is restarted at the spot where the ball was last touched by a player on the opposing team). Games are 15 points; teams switch goals at 8 points.

VARIATIONS: 1. Do not use goalkeepers.
2. A team scores 2 points for a head goal.
3. Restrict the number of touches.

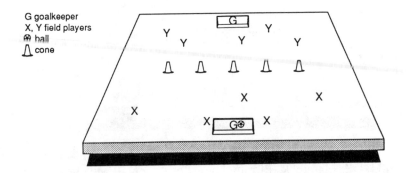

CONTRIBUTOR: Steve Berecz, Boys' Coach, Trumbull High School, Trumbull, Connecticut

Six vs. Four Keep-Away

FOCUS	AREA	PERSONNEL	EQUIPMENT
Passing	20 × 20 yards	10 players	1 ball
Defense			4 cones
			4 vests

FORMATION: One attacker is in the middle of the playing area. Five other attackers, one with a ball, are spread around the area's boundaries. Four defenders wearing vests are located anywhere in the area.

PROCEDURE: The six attackers play two-touch keep-away against the four defenders. If a defender wins the ball, the ball is immediately returned to the attackers. Every 2 minutes four attackers change positions with the defenders, and a new attacker goes into the middle. The object is for the attackers to make as many consecutive passes as possible. The middle attacker counts the passes and a defender counts the number of offensive breakdowns in each 2-minute period. Each group tries to beat the best number.

VARIATIONS: 1. Vary the size of the playing area.
2. Play with a one-touch restriction.
3. Add another attacker.
4. Vary the defensive tempo.

A attacker
D defender
⊕ ball
⨇ cone

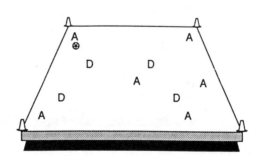

CONTRIBUTOR: John Rennie, Men's Coach, Duke University, Durham, North Carolina

Skill Builder

FOCUS	AREA	PERSONNEL	EQUIPMENT
Control Fitness	20 × 40 yards	15 players	10 balls

FORMATION: Ten feeders about 10 yards apart from each other, each with a ball, form a gauntlet on both sides of a 20 × 40 yard grid. Five other players (X) are lined up at one end of the grid.

PROCEDURE: Each of the X players starts at the top of the grid and runs through the gauntlet, working on the same skill with each feeder. Each X player receives a pass from the feeder, controls the ball as designated, passes back to the feeder, and changes direction to move on to the next feeder. The next player in line begins when the first player reaches the third feeder. After each run the players return to the line and begin another run, working on a different skill. The skills used are (a) inside-of-foot control, (b) instep control, (c) thigh control, (d) chest control, (e) head control, and (f) heading. After all X players complete six skills they exchange positions with five feeders. The drill continues until all 15 players run the gauntlet.

VARIATIONS: 1. Use both legs.
2. Thigh, chest, and head controls must be played in the air.

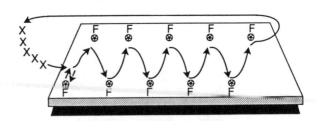

CONTRIBUTOR: Dr. Craig Butcher, Men's Coach, Santa Rosa Junior College, Santa Rosa, California

Stopper Bomb

FOCUS	AREA	PERSONNEL	EQUIPMENT
Attack	1/2 field	3 players	1 ball
			1 goal

FORMATION: D1, the stopper back, is at midfield with a ball. Two other defenders, D2 and D3, are behind midfield to the left and right of D1.

PROCEDURE: D2 runs diagonally to the right to receive a pass from D1. D2 continues in this direction with the ball and passes in the opposite direction to D3, who has made a diagonal run to the left. D3 carries the ball outside and downfield and crosses the ball to D1, who has made a straight run toward the goal. D1 takes a first-time shot on goal.

VARIATIONS: 1. Add players to mark D1, D2, and D3.
2. Add a goalkeeper.

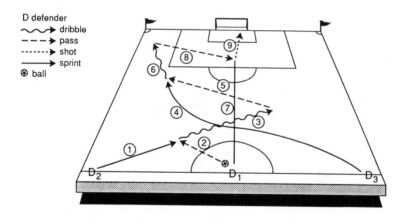

CONTRIBUTOR: Ernest Unger, Boys' Coach, Paramus High School, Paramus, New Jersey

Successive Wall Passing

FOCUS	AREA	PERSONNEL	EQUIPMENT
Passing	Three 20 × 20	5 players	1 ball
Defense	yard grids		3 vests

FORMATION: Two attackers with one ball position themselves at the top of a 20 × 20 yard grid. One defender is positioned on the far line of each of the three grids. Each defender wears a vest.

PROCEDURE: The attackers attempt to beat each defender with two vs. one wall passes, overlaps, or one vs. one dribbling. The ball must be dribbled over the end line of each grid. As soon as the attackers enter each grid, the defender, who must stay on the end line until then, sprints toward the attackers and attempts to delay the attack.

VARIATIONS: 1. Award the attackers 1 point for making it through each grid.
2. Set a time limit for attackers to get through the grids.

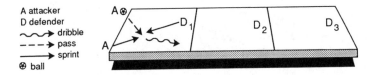

A attacker
D defender
〜〜➤ dribble
‒ ‒ ➤ pass
——➤ sprint
⊕ ball

CONTRIBUTOR: Amy Freeman, Women's Coach, Earlham College, Richmond, Indiana

Support

FOCUS	AREA	PERSONNEL	EQUIPMENT
Support	Varies with	5 players	1 ball
Passing	player level		
Possession			

FORMATION: Four players (numbered X1, X2, X3, and X4) are spread in a rectangular area. X1 has a ball. A defender is in the middle of the area.

PROCEDURE: Players must pass in sequence from 1 to 4. The player next in sequence must anticipate (read) how and at what angle the pass will be received by the preceding player, as well as the angle of the defenders to create good passing opportunities for the passer.

VARIATIONS: 1. Players can pass in reverse order (4 to 1).
2. Limit the number of touches.
3. Add additional defenders and attackers to a maximum of five vs. three.

X field player
D defender
– – – ▶ pass
———▶ sprint
⊕ ball

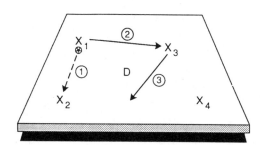

CONTRIBUTOR: Hank Leung, Women's Coach, George Mason University, Fairfax, Virginia

Support of Challenging Player

FOCUS	AREA	PERSONNEL	EQUIPMENT
Defense	20 × 20 yards	4 players	1 ball
Support			

FORMATION: Two attackers (A1 and A2) are about 10 yards apart within the grid. A1 has a ball. Two defenders (D1 and D2) are in proper defensive position; D1 challenges A1, and D2 supports at a 45-degree angle midway between the attackers.

PROCEDURE: A1 passes to A2. On the pass, D2 takes a close position to pressure A2, with D1 moving to the supporting position. When A2 immediately passes the ball back to A1, D1 sprints to pressure A1, with D2 moving to the supporting position.

VARIATIONS: 1. At first, attackers control the ball for 2 or 3 seconds before passing it.
2. Allow one-touch passes only.

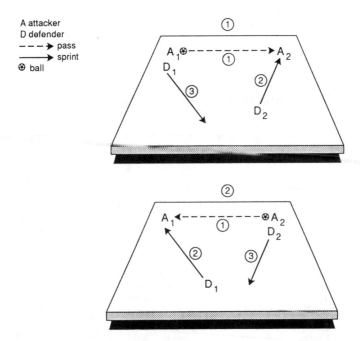

CONTRIBUTOR: Dumitru Oltean, Boys' Coach, Cypress Creek High School, Houston, Texas

Sweeper Clearing

FOCUS	AREA	PERSONNEL	EQUIPMENT
Clearing	1/2 field	8 players	6 balls
Control			4 cones
			1 goal

FORMATION: Two sweepers are on the goal line, one on each side of the goal. Each defender has three balls. Six attackers (forwards or half-backs) are on the sidelines near midfield, three on each side. Two cones about 2 yards apart are on each side of the field by the attackers.

PROCEDURE: Each sweeper dribbles one ball to an area in the goal box and accurately clears the ball to an attacker moving into the area between the cones. The attacker receives the ball and dribbles off the field. The sweeper then clears a second ball past the cones, where the second attacker is moving into position to receive the ball. The sweeper makes a third clear at an increased distance. Both sweepers move at the same time. After all the balls are cleared, sweepers switch sides.

VARIATION: Have attackers dribble downfield, pass back to the sweeper, and sprint into position to receive the clear.

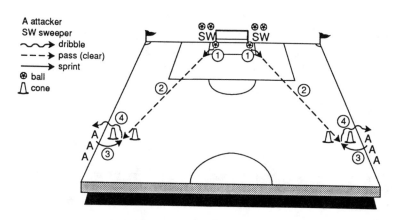

CONTRIBUTOR: Cathy Benton, Women's Coach, Denison University, Granville, Ohio

Switch Ball

FOCUS	AREA	PERSONNEL	EQUIPMENT
Passing	30 × 30 yards	10 to 12	5 balls
Receiving		players	
Movement			
with/without			
the ball			

FORMATION: Three players are in the middle of a 30 × 30 yard grid. The remaining players make a circle around the grid. Five of these players each have a ball.

PROCEDURE: Each player in the middle moves to a player with a ball, receives it, turns, and switches it to a teammate across the field who does not have a ball. Play continues in this fashion for a designated period.

VARIATIONS:
1. Allow two touches for the players in the middle.
2. The switched ball has to be chipped in the air.
3. Add a defender to mark players in the middle.
4. Rotate middle and circle players.

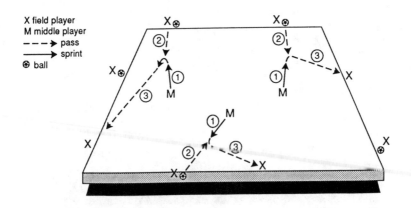

X field player
M middle player
– – –▸ pass
———▸ sprint
⊕ ball

CONTRIBUTOR: Lenny Armuth, Women's Coach, Kean College, Union, New Jersey

Talk to Each Other

FOCUS	AREA	PERSONNEL	EQUIPMENT
Communi-cation	Full field	5 players	1 ball 2 goals

FORMATION: A defender, three midfielders, and an attacker are positioned within the field as shown in the diagram. The defender has a ball.

PROCEDURE: The defender makes a line pass to an outside midfielder, M1, who has called for the ball by saying "line." M1 passes square to M2, who has called "square." The attacker moves to receive a pass from M2 and says "here." The attacker passes diagonally back to M3, who has said "drop." M3 passes to the weak-side midfielder, M1, who says "change." M1 finishes with a cross to the far post for the attacker to shoot first time on goal.

VARIATIONS: 1. Add defenders and a goalkeeper.
2. Use one- or two-touch restrictions.

A attacker
D defender
M midfielder
– – –➤ pass
------➤ shot
——➤ sprint
⊕ ball

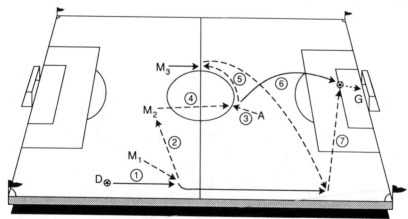

CONTRIBUTOR: Ted Eskildsen, Women's Coach, Grinnell College, Grinnell, Iowa

Target Training

FOCUS	AREA	PERSONNEL	EQUIPMENT
Attack	1/2 field	10 players	2 balls
			4 cones
			2 goals

FORMATION: Two goalkeepers and eight field players are positioned in a half-field area as follows:

1. One goalie (G) is in each goal; a portable goal is at midfield.
2. Four players (X1-X4) are in a square marked by cones in the middle of the area.
3. One player is at one corner of the area and another is in the diagonally opposite corner (X5 and X7). Each of these players has a ball.
4. One target player is just outside each penalty area (X6 and X8).

PROCEDURE: X5 passes to X1, who passes to X2. X2 passes to X5, who has made a timed run to receive the pass. X5 makes a final pass to target player X6, who shoots on goal. X5 and X6 switch positions. Simultaneously, X7 passes to X4, who passes to X3, who provides the outlet pass to X7, and so on. Corner and target players rotate positions continuously.

VARIATIONS:
1. Players in the square interchange positions during play.
2. Center players rotate positions with cover and target players.

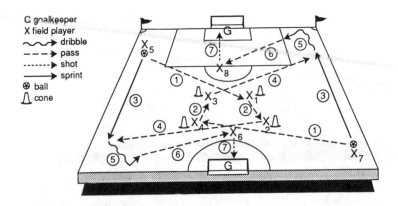

CONTRIBUTOR: Jean Paul Verhees, Women's Coach, University of California at Berkeley, Berkeley, California

Ten vs. Ten
Take It Back

FOCUS	AREA	PERSONNEL	EQUIPMENT
Attack	1/2 field	21 players	1 ball
Defense			1 goal
Transition			10 vests

FORMATION: Two teams are placed on half the field—one attacking the goal and the other on defense. One team wears vests. The goalkeeper, who plays for both teams, is in the goal. One attacker has a ball.

PROCEDURE: Each team attempts to score using the following rules:

1. If the defenders gain possession they must work the ball out until they cross midfield with possession, after which they become the attacking team.
2. If the attackers lose possession, they must work to prevent the defending team from crossing midfield; if they gain possession by doing so, they can immediately attack the goal.
3. All other rules for corner kicks, goal kicks, throw-ins, and so on apply.

VARIATIONS: 1. Limit the number of touches.
2. Reduce the size of the playing area and number of players (e.g., three vs. three in penalty area).
3. Put a time limit on clearance of the zone.

A attacker
D defender
G goalkeeper
⊕ ball

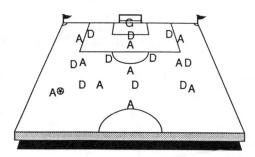

CONTRIBUTOR: David Fall, Men's Coach, Rollins College, Winter Park, Florida

Three-Ball Finishing

FOCUS	AREA	PERSONNEL	EQUIPMENT
Shooting	25 × 15 yards	6 players	12 balls
Goalkeeping		2 feeders	1 goal

FORMATION: Five players, each with a ball, line up 25 yards from the goal. A feeder stands by each goal post with the remaining balls. A goalkeeper is in the goal.

PROCEDURE: The first player in line dribbles a few yards and shoots at the goal. The player continues farther to shoot a quick pass from the left post feeder. After the second shot is taken, the player sprints to head on goal a ball thrown to him or her from the right post feeder. The shooter retrieves his or her shots and then goes to the end of the attack line. After all three shots have been taken, the next player in line begins.

VARIATION: Different types of balls may be served: bouncing, rolling, and so on.

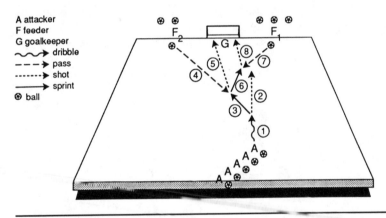

CONTRIBUTOR: Michael Getman, Men's Coach, Harvard University, Cambridge, Massachusetts

Three-Minute Shooting Game

FOCUS	AREA	PERSONNEL	EQUIPMENT
Shooting	1/2 field and	12 players	5 balls
Goalkeeping	area behind		2 cones
Clearing	goal		1 goal

FORMATION: The group is divided into two teams with one goalkeeper for each team. One team spreads out behind the goal area with the goalkeeper in the goal. The other team lines up at midfield. Each player has a ball. Cones are set at the edge of the penalty area as shot markers.

PROCEDURE: Each team is given 3 minutes on attack and 3 minutes on defense. Each attacker in turn runs with the ball on goal and must shoot before or at the line marked by the cones. As soon as a player shoots, the next player in line starts on goal. If the ball is shot wide of the goal, the defenders behind the goal must play the ball back and wide to the field of play before it stops dead. If the ball stops dead, 1 point is given to the attacking team. However, the defending team gets 1 point if they individually or collectively clear the ball or get two touches on the ball before it touches the ground. The attacking team scores 1 point for each goal scored. After 3 minutes teams switch roles.

VARIATIONS: 1. The coach can serve the ball to the attackers at varying heights and angles before they start on goal.
2. Cones can be placed at varying distances from the goal to create different choices for the goalkeeper and shooters.
3. Younger players can be given 1 point for a ball shot on target and 2 points for a goal.

A attacker
D defender
G goalkeeper
〜➤ dribble
------➤ shot
⊕ ball
∆ cone

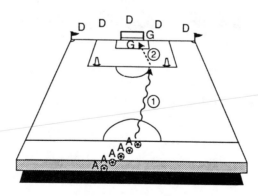

CONTRIBUTOR: Aliceana Wilbur, Women's Coach, William Smith College, Genova, New York

Three Plus One Shooting

FOCUS	AREA	PERSONNEL	EQUIPMENT
Shooting	2 penalty areas	16 players	10 balls
Attack			2 goals
			4 vests

FORMATION: There are two teams of five players each. One team wears colored vests. Three players and a goalkeeper from each team and the opposing team's striker are in each penalty area. Two feeders, each with a supply of balls, are on opposite sides of midfield. Two retrievers are behind each goal.

PROCEDURE: A feeder serves a ball to one team to begin the drill. The field players can serve the ball to their striker in the other area, combine with the striker on attack opportunities, or shoot on goal from the far penalty area. Shots can only be taken from within the near penalty area by the striker. The strikers work for an attack opportunity by pressuring the field players. As soon as an attack is finished, a new ball is served to the team previously on defense.

F feeder
G goalkeeper
R retriever
S striker
X, Y field players
– – –➤ pass
✪ ball

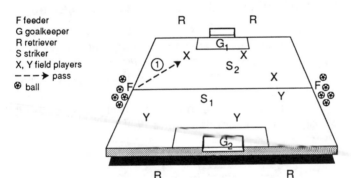

CONTRIBUTOR: Diane R. Boettcher, Women's Coach, Davidson College, Davidson, North Carolina

Three vs. Three Plus Two

FOCUS	AREA	PERSONNEL	EQUIPMENT
Passing	15 × 15 yards	8 players	1 ball
Movement with/without the ball			8 vests

FORMATION: Two teams, X and Y, of three players each and two other players (Z1 and Z2) are within a 15 × 15 yard grid. Each group wears different colored vests. X1 has a ball.

PROCEDURE: Play begins with X1 in control of the ball. The two Z players create a five vs. three situation by playing with the set of three players that has possession. When the five lose possession, the Z players then play with the other three players.

VARIATIONS:
1. Restrict passing to two touches, one touch.
2. Rotate players.
3. Increase the numbers (e.g., four vs. four plus two, five vs. five plus three) and enlarge the playing area accordingly.

X, Y, Z field players
⊕ ball

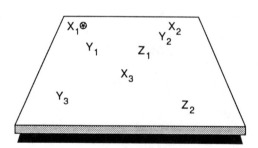

CONTRIBUTOR: Brian McManus, Women's Coach, University of California at San Diego, San Diego, California

Through Ball Passing

114

FOCUS	AREA	PERSONNEL	EQUIPMENT
Passing Movement with/without the ball	20 × 20 yards	5 players	1 ball

FORMATION: Four field players mark the boundaries of a 20 × 20 yard grid. A fifth player, X1, with a ball is between two of the field players.

PROCEDURE: X1 begins the drill with a pass to X2, who sprints to meet the ball and lays it off first time for X1, who has come in support. X2 then turns away, looking for a through pass as X1 plays the ball ahead for X2 to collect and give to X3. X1 now sets up between X2 and X3. X3 repeats the drill, with X4 coming to meet the ball before looking for a through pass and passing the ball to X5. The drill continues around the grid in this fashion.

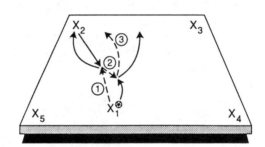

CONTRIBUTOR: Jerry Harbak, Men's Coach, Case Western Reserve University, Cleveland, Ohio

Transition

FOCUS	AREA	PERSONNEL	EQUIPMENT
Transition	15 × 15 yards	8 players	7 balls
			4 cones

FORMATION: Cones set 1 yard apart serve as goals at each end of a 15 × 15 yard grid. Two players—one each from team X and team Y, and one with a ball—are in the center of the grid. Two lines of three players each are at diagonally opposite corners. Each player has a ball.

PROCEDURE: Play one vs. one in the grid. Play is continuous until the ball goes over the end line or a goal is scored. The defender is out, and the first player in line at the end at which the ball went through the goal or over the line attacks the opposite goal against the remaining player. Play continues until one player scores five goals.

VARIATION: Add players in the middle—for example, two vs. two, three vs. three.

X, Y field players
⊕ ball
∏ cone

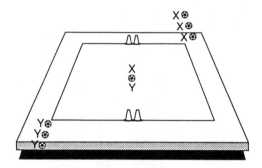

CONTRIBUTOR: S. Page Cotton, Men's Coach, DePauw University, Greencastle, Indiana

Turn, Run, Shoot

FOCUS	AREA	PERSONNEL	EQUIPMENT
Shooting	Penalty area	11 players	15 balls
Fitness		1 feeder	1 cone
			1 goal

FORMATION: A cone is placed in the middle of the penalty area 10 to 12 yards from the goal. A feeder with 15 balls stands outside the goal area facing the goalkeeper. A field player, facing the feeder, stands between the cone and the feeder. The remaining players are behind the goal and serve as retrievers.

PROCEDURE: The feeder pushes the ball forward on either side of the cone. The field player turns, runs to the ball, and shoots first time with the outside foot. As soon as each shot is taken, the player sprints back around the cone to shoot the next ball pushed forward by the feeder. The drill continues until the player has taken 15 shots. After each 15 shots, a new player becomes the shooter.

VARIATIONS: 1. The feeder can make different passes, such as half volleys and volleys.
   2. Rotate the feeder.

F feeder
G goalkeeper
X field player
– – – ▶ pass
------▶ shot
———▶ sprint
⊕ ball
∏ cone

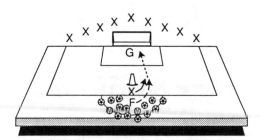

CONTRIBUTOR: Mike Perko, Assistant Boys' Coach, Chatham High School, Chatham, New Jersey

Two-Half-Grid Match

FOCUS	AREA	PERSONNEL	EQUIPMENT
Attack	36 × 44 yards	10 players	10 balls
Defense		1 coach	4 cones
Transition			2 goals
			5 vests

FORMATION: Two defenders and two attackers are in each half of the grid with a goalkeeper in each goal. The boundaries of the grid are marked by cones. The defenders in one half are the teammates of the two attackers in the other half. One team wears colored vests. The coach serves balls from the side.

PROCEDURE: The coach serves a ball onto the field, and players play two vs. two in one half of the grid. Players are usually restricted to their half of the field. However, if the goalkeeper or a defender makes a pass to an attacker on his or her team, either defender can join the attackers, creating a three vs. two on goal. Players off the ball can make a one-for-one switch at any time at midfield (i.e., a defender can switch with an attacker).

VARIATIONS:
1. Restrict players to their own halves with no switching.
2. Use the goalkeeper more offensively. When the goalkeeper receives the ball he or she must get it to the ground immediately and play it with the feet.
3. Allow only three passes in the defensive half; then the ball must be played to the offensive half.
4. Two coaches can alternate serves from opposite sides.

A attacker
C coach
D defender
G goalkeeper
⊛ ball
⌂ cone

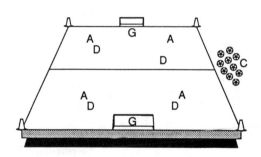

CONTRIBUTOR: Thomas Goodman, Boys' Coach, Suffield High School, Suffield, Connecticut

Two vs. One vs. One vs. One

FOCUS	AREA	PERSONNEL	EQUIPMENT
Defense	10 × 10 grids	5 players	1 ball
Attack			

FORMATION: Two attackers, A1 and A2, one with a ball, and one defender (D1) are in the first 10 × 10 yard grid. Two other defenders, D2 and D3, are in the second and third grids, respectively.

PROCEDURE: A1 and A2 attack D1. When the attackers advance into the second grid they attack D2, and so on until all three defenders have been active. If defenders win the ball attackers start again at the first grid.

VARIATIONS: Attacking players use a two-touch restriction.

A attacker
D defender
⊕ ball

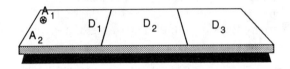

CONTRIBUTOR: David Wright, Men's Coach, Gettysburg College, Gettysburg, Pennsylvania

Vision in Attack

FOCUS	AREA	PERSONNEL	EQUIPMENT
Attack	1/2 field	2 players	1 ball
Defense		1 feeder	1 goal
Vision			

FORMATION: A feeder with a ball is at midfield. An attacker is approximately 20 yards from the feeder, and a defender is on the goal line facing the feeder.

PROCEDURE: The feeder serves the ball on the ground or in the air. The defender can come off or stay on the line when the ball is served. The attacker looks quickly over his or her shoulder as the ball is served and then decides whether to move to the ball to shield it, create space, and take D on; or to turn immediately and take D on. A point is scored when A succeeds at "looking first" and then beating D to the goal line.

VARIATIONS: 1. Allow a return pass to the feeder and a two vs. one attack.
2. Play with a goal and a goalkeeper.
3. Play three vs. three with the restriction that possession is lost if players fail to look for defenders before receiving the ball.

A attacker
F feeder
D defender
∿⇀ dribble
--→ pass
──→ sprint
⊕ ball

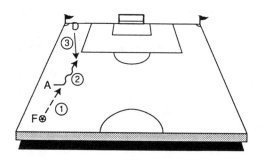

CONTRIBUTOR: Len Bilous, Soccer Magic Camps, Easton, Pennsylvania

Volley Shots to Goalkeeper

FOCUS	AREA	PERSONNEL	EQUIPMENT
Goalkeeping	Penalty area	6 players	5 balls
Shooting		1 coach	1 goal

FORMATION: Five attackers position themselves in an arc about 18 yards from the goal. The goalkeeper is in the net facing the attackers. The coach stands behind the net with five balls.

PROCEDURE: With the goalkeeper facing the attackers, the coach throws a ball over the goalpost to an attacker, who volley kicks the ball in an attempt to score a goal. The goalkeeper is not permitted to turn around to see when or where the coach is throwing the ball.

VARIATIONS: 1. Volley kicks must be played on one bounce.
2. Attackers take head shots on goal.

A attacker
C coach
G goalkeeper
– – –➤ pass
·······➤ shot
⊕ ball

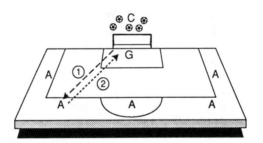

CONTRIBUTOR: Robert Chenevert, Boys' Coach, Algonquin Regional High School, Northboro, Massachusetts

Warm-Up

FOCUS	AREA	PERSONNEL	EQUIPMENT
Warm-up	20 × 20 yards	7 players	1 ball
Passing			4 cones
Fitness			

FORMATION: The team is divided into groups of seven players, each group working in a 20 × 20 yard grid marked by four cones. Players are numbered 1 to 7. X1 has a ball.

PROCEDURE: Players progressively pass the ball in numerical order (X1 to X2 to X3, etc.). The player passing the ball (X1) dribbles to the boundary line of the grid while at the same time the player who will receive the pass (X2) runs to the opposite boundary line. Both players turn back into the grid and approach each other in a direct line. X1 makes a pass (10 or more yards long) to X2, who asks for the ball using whatever words or signs your team uses (e.g., ''yes'' or ''support''). The players not directly involved run in any direction around the perimeter of the grid until it is their turn to enter the grid.

VARIATIONS: 1. Play one touch only.
2. The player receiving the pass turns 180 degrees and dribbles away.
3. Use two balls, with X1 and X4 starting the progression.

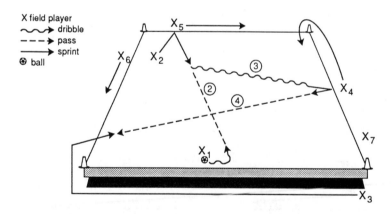

CONTRIBUTOR: Christopher Malone, Women's Coach, SUNY College at Cortland, Cortland, New York

Wing Cross

FOCUS	AREA	PERSONNEL	EQUIPMENT
Passing	1/2 field	8 players	5 balls
Shooting			1 goal
Fitness			

FORMATION: Five players, each with a ball, are at midfield in a straight line facing the goal. One player is 30 yards from the goal on the left wing and one player is 25 yards from the goal on the right wing. A goalkeeper is in the goal.

PROCEDURE: The first player at midfield passes to the left wing. The left wing passes across the 18-yard area to the player moving in from the right wing for a shot on goal. No dribble should be allowed. The player taking the shot should start moving when the pass from the left wing is about to be made. The player making the first pass moves to the right wing position, the right wing moves to the left wing position, and the left wing moves to the end of the passing line.

VARIATIONS: 1. Start play on the right. The left wing becomes the shooter.
2. Allow two dribbles by each player.
3. Use both ends of the field. Add more players.

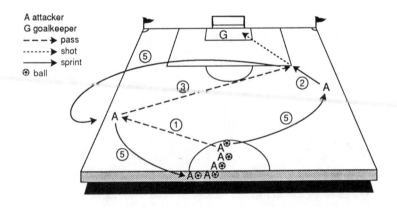

CONTRIBUTOR: Cottrell D. Noel, Men's Coach, University of Massachusetts, Boston, Massachusetts

Wing Service

FOCUS	AREA	PERSONNEL	EQUIPMENT
Attack	50 × 50 yards	12 players	1 ball
Passing			10 cones
			2 goals
			4 vests

FORMATION: Two teams, each with four players and a goalkeeper, and two wings who will play for both teams are within a 50 × 50 yard area. One team wears vests. A goal is on each end line with a goalkeeper in each goal. Two free zones, marked by cones, run the length of the area 5 yards within each sideline. A player on one team has a ball.

PROCEDURE: Play is four vs. four, with the wings always on the attacking team. When one team wins possession they must get the ball to either one of the wings in the free zone. The wings are the only players allowed in the free zone and must stay in the free zone. Goals must come from a ball served by a wing. All players must play two touch except for the wings.

VARIATIONS: 1. Play one touch.
2. Put a defender in the free zone so that a wing must beat a defender before serving the ball.
3. Allow wings to dribble the ball out of the free zone into the center area after receiving the ball in the free zone.

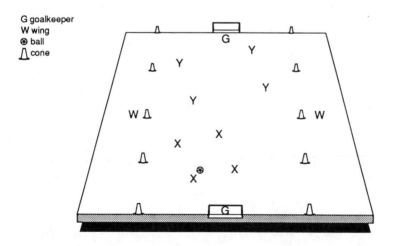

G goalkeeper
W wing
⊕ ball
⌂ cone

CONTRIBUTOR: John T. Rootes, Men's Coach, New Hampshire College, Manchester, New Hampshire

W-M Passing Drill

FOCUS	AREA	PERSONNEL	EQUIPMENT
Passing	Full field	12 players	2 balls
Shooting			2 goals
Goalkeeping			
Fitness			

FORMATION: Using the entire field, players are positioned as follows:

1. One on the left of each goal kick line; each of these players has a ball
2. One on each sideline at each quarter field
3. One on each side of the midfield circle
4. One outside the middle of each penalty area
5. A goalkeeper in each goal

PROCEDURE: Play begins with simultaneous passes from the players on the penalty area line to the nearest sideline players. After each pass, the players then sprint to the next position on that side. The players on top of the penalty area shoot the ball on goal. After each shot on goal, play begins again with a new player in each position.

VARIATIONS:
1. Start play in the opposite direction (right side of goal area).
2. Use two balls on each side (four altogether). The second pass starts when the first ball has reached midfield.

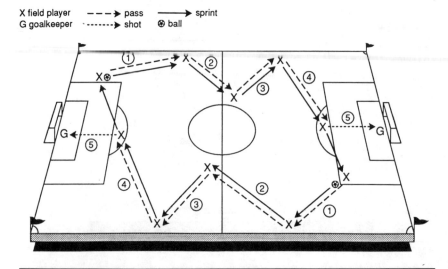

CONTRIBUTOR: Clayton Lewis, Boys' Coach, Farmington High School, Farmington, New Hampshire

Zonal Attacking Soccer

FOCUS	AREA	PERSONNEL	EQUIPMENT
Attack	Full field	22 players	8 balls
Defense		2 coaches	4 cones
			2 goals
			10 vests

FORMATION: Cones divide the full field into attacking, midfield, and defending thirds. The players from each of two teams are positioned as follows: three attackers in each attacking third, four defenders in each defending third, three midfielders in the middle third, and a goalkeeper in each goal. A coach is on each sideline with a supply of balls. Players must stay in their own zones; however, a player who passes a ball across a zone can advance and create a two vs. one situation.

PROCEDURE: A coach distributes a ball to any player. Either coach can similarly distribute the ball after shots over the goal or balls over the touchlines. Defenders are restricted to two-touch passing and midfielders to three-touch; attackers have unrestricted touches.

VARIATIONS: 1. A midfielder playing the ball into the attacking third can have someone else go forward (creating mobility on the attack).
2. Place the emphasis on backs by making long passes to attackers with midfielders running to support the attack.

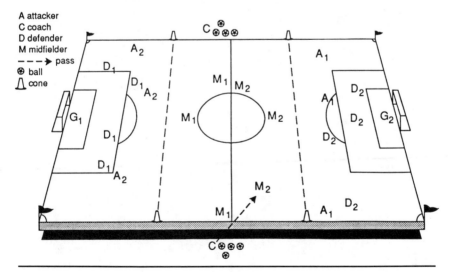

A attacker
C coach
D defender
M midfielder
– – –▶ pass
⊕ ball
⨅ cone

CONTRIBUTOR: Tim Schum, Men's Coach, SUNY at Binghamton, Binghamton, New York

Contributing Authors

Contributor	Institution	Drill number
Steve Allison	Alfred University	85
Lenny Armuth	Kean College	106
Bill Barfield	The Citadel	6
Joe Bean	Wheaton College	94
Cathy Benton	Denison University	105
Steve Berecz	Trumbull High School	98
Jeffrey L. Bickley	Marion, Ohio	42
Len Bilious	Soccer Magic Camps	119
James R. Birmingham	Meadowbrook High School	97
Diane R. Boettcher	Davidson College	112
John Boles	Temple University	54
Efrain Borja	Elizabeth High School	7
Jim Braun	Naperville Central High School	41
Richard Burns	Mount Holyoke College	59
Craig Butcher	Santa Rosa Junior College	100
Brian Chafin	Centre College	26
Robert Chenevert	Algonquin Regional High School	120
Gene Chyzowych	Columbia High School	32
Joe Collins	Indian Hills High School	24
Gus Constantine	New York University	89
Daniel Coombs	Loyola Academy	11
S. Page Cotton	DePauw University	115
Bill Coulthart	Jacksonville University	87
Michael Coven	Brandeis University	72
Ron Crawford	University of Southwestern Louisiana	66
Denise Dallamora	Brandeis University	57
George D. Danner	Griffin High School	40
Rick Dell	Trenton State College	43
J. Kevin Denson	Kempsville High School	14
Bob Dikranian	Southern Connecticut State University	70
Anson Dorrance	University of North Carolina	12
Robert Dubiel	Northampton High School	16
Joseph Eck	Sangamon State University	56
Ted Eskildsen	Grinnell College	107
Roger Essmann	Earlville High School	33
Russ Fager	Rider College	88
David Fall	Rollins College	109

Contributor	Institution	Drill number
Jim Felix	SUNY at Stony Brook	3
Harry Fleishman	Shady Side Academy	71
Amy Freeman	Earlham College	102
Ted Garber	University of New Hampshire	93
Jay Gavitt	Columbia High School	48
Fred Genge	Peoria High School	95
Michael Getman	Harvard University	110
Daniel Gilmore	Glassboro State College	51
Thomas Goodman	Suffield High School	117
T. Barry Gorman	Pennsylvania State University	75
Bob Gray	Alderson Broaddus College	62
Tom Griffith	Princeton University	46
Larry M. Gross	North Carolina State University	77
Jerry Harbak	Case Western Reserve University	114
Buddy Hayford	Wilmington High School	37
Schellas Hyndman	Southern Methodist University	21
I.M. Ibrahim and Greg Hooks	Clemson University	96
Alan Kirkup	Southern Methodist University	27
Loren E. Kline	University of Delaware	8
TJ Kostecky	New Jersey Tech	81
Curtis Lauber	Swarthmore College	69
Hank Leung	George Mason University	103
Clayton Lewis	Farmington High School	124
Stephen Locker	University of Rochester	1
Karen Lombardo	Florissant Valley Community College	34
Lenny Long	Lock Haven University	25
Joe Luxbacher	University of Pittsburgh	79
Joseph A. Machnik	No. 1 Goalkeepers Camp	49
Jack Mackenzie	Quincy College	15
John Makuvek	Moravian College	2
Christopher Malone	SUNY College at Cortland	121
Joseph Mancarella	Monroe Community College	52
Jay Martin	Ohio Wesleyan University	22
Tom Martin	James Madison University	36
Dave Masur	Montclair State College	29
Peter Matischak	Seton Hall University	4
Randall May	Cornell University	73
C. Cliff McCrath	Seattle Pacific University	9
Brian McManus	University of California at San Diego	113
Darryl Metcalfe	Westfield High School	58

Contributor	Institution	Drill number
Jay Miller	University of South Florida	10
Michael C. Mooney	SUNY College at Geneseo	20
Michelle Morgan	Amherst College	68
Vernon Mummert	Drew University	63
Nick Mykulak	Stevens Tech	17
Ed Nirrengarten	Avon High School	91
Cottrell D. Noel	University of Massachusetts	122
Dumitru Oltean	Cypress Creek High School	104
Bret Owensby	Concordia College	65
Gary Parsons	Oakland University	61
Mike Perko	Chatham High School	116
George Perry III	St. Bonaventure University	5
Jack Poland	University of North Carolina at Greensboro	13
Ata Razani and Biren Hodges	Northglenn High School	76
Francis X. Reidy	Saint Leo College	83
John Rennie	Duke University	99
John T. Rootes	New Hampshire College	123
Mike Rubesch	Emory University	74
Ronald R. Rudland	Western High School	92
Susan Ryan	SUNY at Stony Brook	84
Luis A. Sagastume	United States Air Force Academy	67
Don A. Scarborough	Brevard College	64
Fred Schmalz	University of Evansville	30
Sigi Schmid	University of California at Los Angeles	44
Tim Schum	SUNY at Binghamton	125
Robby Searl	Nazareth College	60
Margie Shade	Ohio Wesleyan University	19
Ronald W. Shewcraft	North Adams State College	39
David Springer	Binghamton High School	28
Karen Stanley	Seattle Pacific University	23
Thomas Taylor	West Essex High School	80
Jeff Tipping	Muhlenberg College	31
Tom Turner	Cleveland State University	90
Ernest Unger	Paramus High School	101
Jeff Vagell	Wesleyan University	38
Jean Paul Verhees	University of California at Berkeley	108
Bill Viger	Wheeler High School	50
Joe Waldron	University of Evansville	35
Bob Warming	Creighton University	55

Contributor	Institution	Drill number
Helmut Werner	Randolph-Macon College	78
John Werner	Arlington Memorial High School	82
Aliceana Wilbur	William Smith College	111
David Wright	Gettysburg College	118
Owen L. Wright	University of La Verne	86
Jack Writer	Cornell University	47
Jerry Yeagley	Indiana University	53
Suzanne Zaloom	Union College	45
Richard G. Zawacki	Don Bosco Prep	18

About the Editors

John Reeves and Malcolm Simon combine more than 50 years of soccer coaching expertise in their newest coach's guide, *Select Soccer Drills*. Two of America's top coaches, Reeves and Simon are the editors of two previous Leisure Press soccer books, *Coaches Collection of Soccer Drills* and *The Soccer Games Book*.

John Reeves has been coaching soccer since 1961 at both the youth and collegiate levels. Currently the director of the Division of Physical Education and Athletics for the State University of New York at Stony Brook, Reeves is a member of the National Soccer Coaches Association of America and is also past-president of the Intercollegiate Soccer Association of America. He earned his doctoral degree in 1983 from Columbia University.

Malcolm Simon is the director of physical education and athletics at the New Jersey Institute of Technology. He has coached soccer, basketball, tennis, and volleyball in college, camp, and YMCA settings since 1954. He coached the 1960 NAIA national champions and the 1961 runners-up. Sixteen of his players have been named All-Americans, and five have gone on to play professional soccer nationally and internationally, including Hernan "Chico" Borja. Simon is a member of the National Soccer Coaches Association of America.

Additional soccer resources

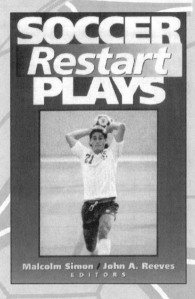

Soccer Restart Plays

J. Malcolm Simon, MA, and John A. Reeves, EdD, Editors

Foreword by Cliff McCrath

1994 • Paperback • 152 pp
Item PSIM0521
ISBN 0-87322-521-X
$14.95 ($21.95 Canadian)

"I don't know of any other source which has compiled so many of the top coaches best set plays. Two thumbs-up for Soccer Restart Plays."

Ed Tremble, MS
U.S. Soccer National Staff Coach
Connecticut Director of Coaching
Adidas National Soccer Advisory Board

Soccer Practice Games

Joe Luxbacher

1995 • Paperback• 152 pp
Item PLUX0554
ISBN 0-87322-554-6
$14.95 ($19.95 Canadian)

"Not just another training guide, but a tool coaches of all age groups can use, over and over again. If you can't run a better practice after reading this, you should consider a different line of work!"

Dan Woog
Executive Editor
Soccer America's Youth Soccer Letter

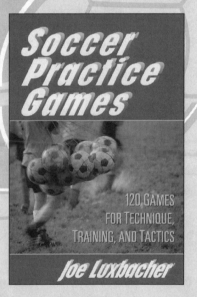

Prices are subject to change.

To place your order: U.S. customers call **TOLL-FREE 1 800 747-4457;**
customers outside of U.S. use the appropriate
telephone number/address shown in the front of this book.

HUMAN KINETICS
The Premier Publisher for Sports & Fitness
www.humankinetics.com